Great Taste ~ Low Fat

PASTA SAUCES

TIME
LIFE
BOOKS

ALEXANDRIA, VIRGINIA

TABLE OF CONTENTS

Lemon Chicken Sauce

~

page 46

Chili Shrimp Sauce

page 105

INTRODUCTION

Our mission at Great Taste~Low Fat is to take the work and worry out of everyday low-fat cooking; to provide delicious, fresh, and filling recipes for family and friends; to use quick, streamlined methods and available ingredients; and, within every recipe, to keep the percentage of calories from fat under 30 percent.

Pasta has been growing in popularity for years, and that's all to the good: It's an incredibly versatile food that supplies energizing carbohydrates and virtually no fat. But it's not just the pasta that we crave, it's the *sauce*. Pasta is like a blank canvas: a neutral base on which to "paint" with colorful, flavorful sauces. And there's an added dimension—a sculptural one, if you will—in that pasta comes in hundreds of shapes. Our chef, Sandra Gluck, has put her culinary and artistic talents to work in developing a repertoire of original pasta sauces that appeal to the eye as well as the palate. With a thought for your busy schedule, Sandy has created sauces that are easy and quick to prepare—but far superior to pasta toppers that come in jars or cans. Almost anyone could make a tasty sauce if healthy eating were not a consideration; Sandy's great skill lies in combining low-fat ingredients in deliciously appealing ways. The recipes are full of fresh vegetables for super nutrition as well as flavor and color. We recommend several pastas for each sauce; by switching shapes, you can vary the dish slightly each time you serve it.

THE ART OF THE SAUCE

The process of inventing pasta sauces begins with access to inspiring ingredients. Sandy's many trips to Italy have impressed her with the importance of using fresh produce in season. "If I've just come back from the farmers' market with an armload of fresh vegetables, I'll review my pasta shelf to see what would go with what. If I've bought eggplant or cauliflower, I'll think about combining those vegetables with a sturdy pasta like radiatore or gnocchi. If I've picked up a head of cabbage, I might decide to toss strips of cabbage with ribbons of fettuccine. I tend to make lots of meatless pasta meals in the summer, and prefer heartier meat sauces in cooler weather." With a family to feed, Sandy will sometimes make a batch of pasta sauce to freeze. "It's good 'insurance' for busy times," she says. "While the pasta cooks, I just reheat the sauce and make a salad."

A RICH SELECTION

Don't think for a moment that all these recipes are Italian. Although there's a full complement of delicious tomato toppings, including Puttanesca, Amatriciana, and Arrabbiata—as well as Alfredo, Primavera, Pesto, and other favorites—you'll also find sauces flavored with curry, almonds, lemon, chili powder, paprika, dill, or mint; and dishes inspired by Thai, Chinese, Indonesian, and Mexican cuisines. Some of the recipes are adaptations of familiar main dishes (or soups) into pasta-sauce among others, chili, minestrone, chicken parmigiana, and pork and beans.

In the first chapter, Poultry Sauces, you'll find fragrant Chicken Sauce with Sage, Turkey Sauce with Orange and Sweet Spices, and a Neapolitan Chicken Sauce with true old-world flavor. In addition to a sturdy Beef and Mushroom Ragù, our Meat Sauces chapter offers Pork Piccata Sauce, Paprikash Sauce, Thai-Style Beef and Peanut Sauce, and a creamy Ham and Ricotta Cheese Sauce. On a lighter note, you'll want to sample our Seafood Sauces, such as Mediterranean Cod Sauce, Provençal Shrimp Sauce, and festive Salmon and Lemon-Dill Sauce. You'll be impressed with the variety of recipes in the Vegetable Sauces chapter. Choices range from lush, creamy sauces—including Artichoke-Parmesan Sauce, Asparagus Cream Sauce, and Vegetable-Cheese Sauce—to highly seasoned Vegetable Agliata (a garlic-lover's delight), Spicy Tomato Sauce, and Green Bean Gremolata Sauce.

Be sure to read the "Secrets of Low-Fat Cooking" pages, which follow, for tips on ingredients, the art of matching pasta shapes to sauces, and pasta cooking techniques. Then you'll be on your way to enjoying a fabulous succession of delicious, low-fat, family-pleasing pasta sauces.

CONTRIBUTING EDITORS

Sandra Rose Gluck, a New York City chef, has years of experience creating delicious low-fat recipes that are quick to prepare. Her secret for satisfying results is to always aim for great taste and variety. By combining readily available, fresh ingredients with simple cooking techniques, Sandra has created the perfect recipes for today's busy lifestyles.

Grace Young has been the director of a major test kitchen specializing in low-fat and health-related cookbooks for over 12 years. Grace oversees the development, taste testing, and nutritional analysis of every recipe in Great Taste~Low Fat. Her goal is simple: take the work and worry out of low-fat cooking so that you can enjoy delicious, healthy meals every day.

Kate Slate has been a food editor for almost 20 years, and has published thousands of recipes in cookbooks and magazines. As the Editorial Director of Great Taste~Low Fat, Kate combined simple, easy to follow directions with practical low-fat cooking tips. The result is guaranteed to make your low-fat cooking as rewarding and fun as it is foolproof.

NUTRITION

Every recipe in *Great Taste~Low Fat* provides per-serving values for the nutrients listed in the chart at right. The daily intakes listed in the chart are based on those recommended by the USDA and presume a nonsedentary lifestyle. The nutritional emphasis in this book is not only on controlling calories, but on reducing total fat grams. Research has shown that dietary fat metabolizes more easily into body fat than do carbohydrates and protein. In order to control the amount of fat in a given recipe and in your diet in general, no more than 30 percent of the calories should come from fat.

Nutrient	Women	Men
Fat	<65 g	<80 g
Calories	2000	2500
Saturated fat	<20 g	<25 g
Carbohydrate	300 g	375 g
Protein	50 g	65 g
Cholesterol	<300 mg	<300 mg
Sodium	<2400 mg	<2400 mg

These recommended daily intakes are averages used by the Food and Drug Administration and are consistent with the labeling on all food products. Although the values for cholesterol and sodium are the same for all adults, the other intake values vary depending on gender, ideal weight, and activity level. Check with a physician or nutritionist for your own daily intake values.

SECRETS OF LOW-FAT COOKING

PASTA SAUCES

Thank goodness for pasta—and for the thousands of wonderful ways to serve it. But without some sort of sauce, pasta would be undeniably dull. Just add a simple sauce (chopped raw tomatoes, fresh basil or oregano, and a shimmer of extra-virgin olive oil, for example), and pasta takes its rightful place as one of the world's great and versatile foods, as welcome at a festive dinner party on Saturday evening as it is at the family supper table any night of the week.

KEYS TO HEALTHFUL SAUCES

A great pasta sauce should cling to the pasta and stick to your ribs—and of course the taste must be memorable. This is as true of a healthful, low-fat sauce as it is of a high-fat one, and for satisfying results, it takes some ingenuity consisting of equal parts cooking technique and knowledge of ingredients. We supply both in our recipes, and offer them to you in these pages. In the photograph at right are key components of great pasta sauces: tomatoes in various forms, hot-shot flavor boosters, and low-fat thickeners that can enrich a sauce. We use them all—and when your kitchen is stocked with these ingredients, you may be tempted to improvise your own original sauces, or cook up variations on the recipes in this book.

FABULOUS FLAVORS

Pasta's unassuming taste is the perfect foil for intense flavorings. The fresh vegetables, lean meats, poultry, and seafood that go into our sauces are artfully enhanced with inventively sassy seasonings. We start by giving our sauces a flavorful foundation: We sizzle up some lean Canadian bacon, steep dried mushrooms in boiling water, or sauté onions, garlic, and bell pepper until they're tender and supremely savory. As the sauce simmers, we make judicious use of other high-flavor ingredients: pungent brine-cured or pimiento-stuffed olives, piquant capers, freshly grated citrus zest, and fragrant spices. For an outstanding finish, we often splash in some wine—a mellow Marsala, nutty sherry, or crisp, dry white—or drizzle in a few drops of fruity, extra-virgin olive oil. Wine vinegar adds full flavor as well as tartness; balsamic vinegar has a uniquely rounded, sweetly mellow taste. We're careful to add fresh herbs, too, when the sauce is nearly cooked, lest they lose their full bouquet.

TASTY TOMATOES

No discussion of pasta sauces would be complete without a mention of tomatoes, which form the basis for so many classic sauces. Among the juiciest and most flavorful of vegetables, tomatoes are a natural for sauce-making. Fresh tomatoes, whether globe or beefsteak, plum or cherry, can be diced, chopped, or puréed to make raw and cooked pasta toppings. The better the tomatoes, the better the sauce—so it's worth hunting down vine-ripened tomatoes at roadside stands and farmers' markets (or in your own backyard, if you have a garden) during the growing season.

Of course, locally grown tomatoes are not available year-round, which is why you'll want to keep ready-to-use tomato products on hand. The canned ones—peeled tomatoes, stewed tomatoes, tomato purées, sauces, and pastes offer consistently good flavor; we use no-salt-added products for delicately seasoned sauces without excessive sodium (check the ingredients on the label since not all cans are labled "no-salt-added"). Don't forget sun-dried tomatoes, with their super-concentrated essence-of-tomato flavor; their pleasant chewiness adds textural interest, too. Use dry-packed tomatoes, rather than oil-packed, for low-fat meals.

THICK AND RICH

Sauces can be thickened in many ways, but if a healthful pasta dinner is your goal, copious quantities of butter, oil, heavy cream, or cheese are not appropriate options. One smart trick that we use in several recipes is to purée or mash all or some of the solid ingredients (such as beans or vegetables) cooked in the sauce. You can do this with a food processor or blender (regular or hand-held), or with a fork or wooden spoon. Another option is adding a starchy ingredient, such as flour or cornstarch, to the sauce. Flour makes a thicker, opaque sauce, while cornstarch produces a lighter, more translucent one. Starchy vegetables such as potatoes or corn can also thicken a sauce slightly with the natural starches they give off while cooking.

Dairy products add inimitable richness to pasta sauces, and even reduced-fat products will do the trick. Among those utilized in our recipes are rich-tasting Neufchâtel, a reduced-fat cream cheese; low-fat and skimmed evaporated milk (smart stand-ins for heavy cream); tangy low-fat and nonfat yogurt; and velvety reduced-fat sour cream. Parmesan and other grated sharp cheeses can also give body to a pasta sauce. Use a well-aged cheese, which will contribute plenty of flavor as well as substance. Naturally, when cooking low-fat meals, you'll want to use full-fat cheeses, such as Parmesan or Cheddar, in moderation.

STRAND PASTAS

STUFFED PASTAS

TUBE PASTAS

SHAPED PASTAS

COOKING PASTA PERFECTLY

You'll enjoy our sauces to the fullest when the pasta itself is cooked to perfection. That means al dente—not soft or limp, but gently resistant when you bite into it. Learn to gauge the proper texture for yourself: Different brands require different cooking times, and fresh pasta cooks much faster than dried. For 10 ounces of pasta, use a large pot—at least 4 quarts—and bring the water to a rolling boil (cover the pot to speed the process). Salt is optional—our recipes don't call for it. Add the pasta, stir to keep it from clumping together, and return to a boil. Check for doneness by biting a piece of pasta. When it's still a bit chewy, but has no white core remaining in the center, the pasta is done. Drain it well in a colander or strainer before adding the sauce.

PASTA PAIRINGS

Venerable traditions govern the suitability of specific pastas to certain sauces; these traditions arise from the size and shape of the pasta as well as the texture and flavor of the sauce. We've observed these "rules" (though not slavishly) in our recipes,

suggesting one or more appropriate pastas for each sauce. For instance, a smooth but clingy sauce is ideal for strand pastas such as spaghetti, long fusilli, and linguine. Stuffed pastas, almost a meal in themselves, don't require complicated sauces, while flat noodles like fettuccine are great with creamy sauces. Tube pastas—ziti and penne, for example—go well with vegetable sauces. Chunky sauces are neatly complemented by what we think of as "sauce-catcher" pastas: shells, ruote (wagon wheels), radiatore, and other shapes with hollows and gaps to hold the sauce. Pasta twists, such as rotini and farfalle (bow ties), are among the most versatile pastas and can be served with a wide variety of sauces. On this page you see pastas grouped according to size and shape, and you can always substitute within a group. But feel free to go beyond the guidelines: If you're out of penne, use fettuccine broken into shorter pieces; if you prefer chewy rigatoni to slippery spaghetti, go ahead and make the switch. If your kids are fond of a certain pasta shape, use the shells, elbows, or whatever they prefer as a way of encouraging them to try different sauces.

POULTRY SAUCES

1

Tossing this colorful stir-fry with pasta—instead of serving it with rice—lends a new twist to an Asian classic. The light sauce, based on cornstarch-thickened broth, melds the pasta, chicken, and crisp-tender vegetables into a harmonious whole. We call for fettuccine, but just about any ribbon-shaped pasta noodle would work in this recipe.

Asian Chicken Sauce

Serves: 4
Working time: 35 minutes
Total time: 35 minutes

10 ounces fettuccine

2 teaspoons vegetable oil

10 ounces skinless, boneless chicken thighs, cut into ½-inch chunks

6 scallions, thinly sliced

2 cloves garlic, minced

1 red bell pepper, cut into ½-inch squares

3 carrots, cut into 2 x ¼-inch julienne strips

¾ teaspoon ground ginger

½ pound snow peas, strings removed (see tip) and halved crosswise

1 cup reduced-sodium chicken broth, defatted

2 tablespoons reduced-sodium soy sauce

¼ teaspoon salt

1½ teaspoons cornstarch mixed with 1 tablespoon water

1. In a large pot of boiling water, cook the pasta until just tender. Drain well.

2. Meanwhile, in a large nonstick skillet, heat the oil until hot but not smoking over medium heat. Add the chicken, scallions, and garlic and cook, stirring, until coated, about 1 minute. Add the bell pepper, carrots, and ginger and cook, stirring frequently, until the chicken and vegetables are just cooked through, about 5 minutes.

3. Add the snow peas to the pan and cook until the snow peas are slightly softened, about 2 minutes. Add the broth, soy sauce, and salt and bring to a boil. Stir in the cornstarch mixture and cook, stirring constantly, until slightly thickened, about 1 minute.

4. Toss the sauce with the hot pasta and serve.

Helpful hint: If you're a big fan of ginger, you could add about 1 tablespoon grated fresh ginger to this recipe (with the ground ginger in step 2).

To prepare fresh snow peas for cooking, trim the stem end and pull off the string along the straight side.

Fat: 8g/16%
Calories: 450
Saturated Fat: 1.6g
Carbohydrate: 65g
Protein: 28g
Cholesterol: 126mg
Sodium: 677mg

TURKEY SAUSAGE AND SPINACH SAUCE

SERVES: 4
WORKING TIME: 30 MINUTES
TOTAL TIME: 30 MINUTES

Pasta with sausage and cream sauce might not sound like a healthy, low-fat main dish, but you may be surprised when you read the ingredients for this recipe. The sausage is made from turkey, the smooth sauce is based on low-fat milk and Neufchâtel (reduced-fat cream cheese), and there's a generous portion of spinach in every serving.

10 ounces shaped pasta, such as farfalle (bow ties) or orecchiette

2 teaspoons olive oil

½ pound Italian-style turkey sausage, casings removed

1 red onion, finely chopped

4 cloves garlic, minced

10-ounce package frozen chopped spinach, thawed and squeezed dry

1 cup evaporated low-fat milk

2 tablespoons reduced-fat cream cheese (Neufchâtel)

¼ teaspoon freshly ground black pepper

⅓ cup grated Parmesan cheese

1. In a large pot of boiling water, cook the pasta until just tender. Drain well.

2. Meanwhile, in a large nonstick skillet, heat the oil until hot but not smoking over medium heat. Crumble in the sausage and cook until no longer pink, about 3 minutes. Add the onion and garlic and cook, stirring frequently, until the onion is softened, about 7 minutes.

3. Stir the spinach into the skillet and cook until heated through, about 2 minutes. Add the milk, cream cheese, and pepper and cook, stirring frequently, until slightly thickened, about 4 minutes.

4. Toss the sauce with the hot pasta and the Parmesan. Divide among 4 bowls and serve.

Helpful hints: To prepare the sausage for this recipe, slit the casings lengthwise with the tip of a sharp knife, then peel off the casings with your fingers. If you can't find evaporated low-fat milk, use evaporated skimmed milk instead.

FAT: 14G/24%
CALORIES: 518
SATURATED FAT: 4.3G
CARBOHYDRATE: 69G
PROTEIN: 29G
CHOLESTEROL: 50MG
SODIUM: 660MG

CHICKEN, PINE NUT, AND BASIL SAUCE

SERVES: 4
WORKING TIME: 20 MINUTES
TOTAL TIME: 30 MINUTES

You know there's a tasty dish in the making when basil and pine nuts are paired. Here, they're puréed with cream cheese and broth to make a delicious sauce. The perfect pasta for such a dish is one that has crevices to catch the sauce—twisty rotini, ruffly radiatore, and cavatappi are some good choices. A crisp salad completes the meal.

10 ounces shaped pasta, such as rotini or radiatore

1 tablespoon olive oil

¾ pound skinless, boneless chicken breasts, cut into ½-inch chunks

2 cloves garlic, minced

13¾-ounce can reduced-sodium chicken broth, defatted

½ cup coarsely chopped sun-dried (not oil-packed) tomatoes

½ teaspoon salt

¼ teaspoon red pepper flakes

¾ cup packed fresh basil leaves

2 tablespoons reduced-fat cream cheese (Neufchâtel)

1 tablespoon pine nuts

1. In a large pot of boiling water, cook the pasta until just tender. Drain well.

2. Meanwhile, in a large nonstick skillet, heat 2 teaspoons of the oil until hot but not smoking over medium heat. Add the chicken and cook, stirring, until browned, about 5 minutes. With a slotted spoon, transfer the chicken to a plate.

3. Add the remaining 1 teaspoon oil and the garlic to the skillet and cook until the garlic is softened, about 1 minute. Add all but ¼ cup of the broth, the sun-dried tomatoes, salt, and red pepper flakes and bring to a boil. Reduce the heat to a simmer and cook until the tomatoes are very soft, about 8 minutes.

4. Meanwhile, in a food processor or blender, combine the reserved ¼ cup broth, the basil, cream cheese, and pine nuts and process to a smooth purée. Stir the purée into the skillet. Return the chicken to the pan and cook until the sauce is smooth and creamy and the chicken is heated through, 2 to 3 minutes. Toss the sauce with the hot pasta, divide among 4 bowls, and serve.

Helpful hint: To store fresh basil, place the stems in a glass or jar of water; cover the leaves loosely with a plastic bag and refrigerate.

FAT: 8G/15%
CALORIES: 471
SATURATED FAT: 1.9G
CARBOHYDRATE: 64G
PROTEIN: 34G
CHOLESTEROL: 53MG
SODIUM: 617MG

CHICKEN SAUCE WITH SAGE

SERVES: 4
WORKING TIME: 20 MINUTES
TOTAL TIME: 40 MINUTES

1 tablespoon olive oil

1 onion, diced

2 cloves garlic, minced

¾ pound ground chicken

½ cup dry white wine

1½ cups reduced-sodium chicken broth, defatted

½ pound cremini or button mushrooms, quartered

2 cups diced plum tomatoes or canned no-salt-added tomatoes, chopped with their juices

1½ teaspoons dried sage

1 small bay leaf

1 teaspoon salt

½ teaspoon sugar

¼ teaspoon freshly ground black pepper

10 ounces shaped pasta, such as medium shells or ruote (wagon wheels)

3 tablespoons grated Parmesan cheese

1. In a large nonstick skillet, heat the oil until hot but not smoking over medium heat. Add the onion and garlic and cook, stirring frequently, until the onion begins to soften, about 4 minutes. Add the chicken and cook, stirring to break up the meat, until the chicken is no longer pink, about 5 minutes.

2. Add the wine to the skillet and cook until almost evaporated, about 1 minute. Add the broth, mushrooms, tomatoes, sage, bay leaf, salt, sugar, and pepper and bring to a boil. Reduce the heat to a simmer, cover, and cook until the sauce is richly flavored and thickened, about 20 minutes.

3. Meanwhile, in a large pot of boiling water, cook the pasta until just tender. Drain well.

4. Toss the sauce with the hot pasta. Divide among 4 plates, sprinkle the Parmesan over, and serve.

Helpful hint: If you like, grind the chicken at home: Cut ¾ pound skinless, boneless chicken breast into chunks and process it in a food processor until finely ground, about 30 seconds.

FAT: 14G/25%
CALORIES: 503
SATURATED FAT: 3.3G
CARBOHYDRATE: 65G
PROTEIN: 29G
CHOLESTEROL: 74MG
SODIUM: 918MG

Pasta, ground meat, and tomatoes can add up to the same old spaghetti dinner—or they can be transformed into something far more interesting. Here, for instance, we use ground chicken and plum tomatoes for a light, fresh-tasting dish. A good measure of aromatic sage adds a Tuscan note.

CHICKEN, PROSCIUTTO, AND ARTICHOKE SAUCE

SERVES: 4
WORKING TIME: 40 MINUTES
TOTAL TIME: 40 MINUTES

For a country-style Italian dinner, we've started with a handful of chopped prosciutto, the super-savory Italian ham that can add rich flavor to a sauce in seconds. The chicken, tomatoes, carrots, and artichokes all benefit from this big-time taste booster. The large lasagna noodles, broken into smaller pieces, resemble squares of country-style homemade pasta.

1 tablespoon olive oil

¼ cup plus 2 tablespoons coarsely chopped prosciutto or Canadian bacon (2 ounces)

2 carrots, quartered lengthwise and thinly sliced

1 rib celery, quartered lengthwise and thinly sliced

10 ounces lasagna noodles, broken crosswise into thirds

9-ounce package frozen artichoke hearts, thawed and coarsely chopped

½ cup dry red wine

1 cup canned no-salt-added tomatoes, chopped with their juices

1 cup reduced-sodium chicken broth, defatted

½ teaspoon salt

¼ teaspoon dried thyme

¾ pound skinless, boneless chicken breasts, cut into ½-inch chunks

1 cup frozen peas

1½ teaspoons cornstarch mixed with 1 tablespoon water

1. In a large nonstick skillet, heat the oil until hot but not smoking over medium heat. Add the prosciutto and cook, stirring frequently, until lightly crisped, about 3 minutes. Add the carrots and celery and cook, stirring frequently, until the carrots are softened, about 5 minutes.

2. In a large pot of boiling water, cook the pasta until just tender. Drain well.

3. Meanwhile, add the artichokes to the skillet and cook, stirring frequently, until the artichokes are tender, about 15 minutes. Add the wine, increase the heat to high, and cook until the wine has almost evaporated, about 2 minutes. Add the tomatoes, broth, salt, and thyme and bring to a boil. Reduce the heat to a simmer, add the chicken, and cook until the chicken is just barely cooked through, about 3 minutes.

4. Add the peas to the skillet, return to a boil, and stir in the cornstarch mixture. Cook, stirring constantly, until the sauce is slightly thickened, about 1 minute. Toss the sauce with the hot pasta, divide among 4 bowls, and serve.

Helpful hint: If you like the flavor of celery, don't throw away the leafy tops. Chop them and use them as a flavoring or garnish, as you would parsley.

FAT: 8G/14%
CALORIES: 510
SATURATED FAT: 1.5G
CARBOHYDRATE: 71G
PROTEIN: 38G
CHOLESTEROL: 61MG
SODIUM: 837MG

19

Sweet and Savory Chicken Sauce

Serves: 4
Working time: 30 minutes
Total time: 35 minutes

Apple, banana, and raisins, combined with chicken in a creamy curry sauce, make an unexpected and delicious pasta topping.

10 ounces shaped pasta, such as small shells or ruote (wagon wheels)

1 tablespoon olive oil

¾ pound skinless, boneless chicken breasts, cut into ½-inch chunks

1 red Delicious apple, cored and diced

1 onion, coarsely diced

2 cloves garlic, minced

1 teaspoon curry powder

1¼ cups reduced-sodium chicken broth, defatted

1 firm-ripe banana, cut into ¼-inch slices

¼ cup golden raisins

¾ teaspoon salt

½ cup evaporated skimmed milk

2 teaspoons cornstarch

2 teaspoons fresh lemon juice

¼ cup chopped fresh parsley

1. In a large pot of boiling water, cook the pasta until just tender. Drain well.

2. Meanwhile, in a large nonstick skillet, heat 2 teaspoons of the oil until hot but not smoking over medium heat. Add the chicken and cook, stirring, until browned, about 5 minutes. With a slotted spoon, transfer the chicken to a plate.

3. Add the remaining 1 teaspoon oil to the skillet. Add the apple, onion, and garlic and cook, stirring, until the onion begins to soften, 4 to 5 minutes. Add the curry powder and cook, stirring, until fragrant, about 30 seconds. Add the broth, banana, raisins, and salt and bring to boil. Reduce to a simmer, cover, and cook until the banana is softened but not mushy, about 5 minutes.

4. In a small bowl, combine the evaporated milk with the cornstarch. Stir the cornstarch mixture into the skillet and cook, stirring constantly, until the sauce is slightly thickened, about 1 minute. Return the chicken to the pan and cook until the chicken is heated through, about 1 minute. Stir in the lemon juice. Toss the sauce with the hot pasta, divide among 4 bowls, sprinkle the parsley over, and serve.

Helpful hint: You can use another favorite apple variety instead of the Delicious apple; pick a red-skinned type for a touch of color.

Fat: 6g/10%
Calories: 517
Saturated Fat: 1g
Carbohydrate: 82g
Protein: 33g
Cholesterol: 51mg
Sodium: 689mg

TURKEY AND BASIL PESTO

SERVES: 4
WORKING TIME: 20 MINUTES
TOTAL TIME: 40 MINUTES

1 tablespoon olive oil

¾ pound skinless, boneless turkey breast, cut into ½-inch chunks

10 ounces all-purpose potatoes, diced

3 cloves garlic, minced

2¼ cups reduced-sodium chicken broth, defatted

1 cup packed fresh basil leaves

½ teaspoon salt

¼ teaspoon freshly ground black pepper

10 ounces egg noodles

10-ounce package frozen peas, thawed

⅓ cup grated Parmesan cheese

¼ cup reduced-fat sour cream

1. In a large nonstick skillet, heat 2 teaspoons of the oil until hot but not smoking over medium heat. Add the turkey and cook, stirring, until browned, about 5 minutes. With a slotted spoon, transfer the turkey to a plate.

2. Add the remaining 1 teaspoon oil to the skillet. Add the potatoes and garlic and cook, stirring, until the garlic is fragrant, about 1 minute. Stir in the broth, basil, salt, and pepper and bring to a boil. Reduce to a simmer, cover, and cook until the potatoes are tender, about 20 minutes.

3. Meanwhile, in a large pot of boiling water, cook the noodles until just tender. Drain well.

4. Transfer the potato-basil mixture to a blender or food processor and process to a smooth purée. Return the purée to the skillet along with the turkey. Add the peas, all but 1 tablespoon of the Parmesan, and the sour cream and cook over medium heat until heated through, about 3 minutes. Toss the sauce with the hot pasta. Divide among 4 bowls, sprinkle with the remaining 1 tablespoon Parmesan, and serve.

Helpful hint: We've used curly egg noodles here, but you can use flat noodles instead.

FAT: 12G/18%
CALORIES: 595
SATURATED FAT: 3.6G
CARBOHYDRATE: 80G
PROTEIN: 43G
CHOLESTEROL: 130MG
SODIUM: 864MG

I nstead of copious quantities of oil, cheese, and nuts, this basil pesto is thickened with puréed potatoes.

CHICKEN AND BASIL-PEPPER CREAM SAUCE

SERVES: 4
WORKING TIME: 25 MINUTES
TOTAL TIME: 25 MINUTES

Roasted red peppers perk up any dish, and there's no reason to go without when you can buy them in jars, all ready to go. (Look for roasted red peppers in the Italian or gourmet foods section of your supermarket.) The peppers are puréed, along with evaporated milk and broth, to make a rosy, robust sauce for pasta, chicken, and green beans.

10 ounces shaped pasta, such as radiatore or rotini

½ pound green beans, cut into 2-inch lengths

1 tablespoon olive oil

¾ pound skinless, boneless chicken breasts, cut into ½-inch chunks

8-ounce jar roasted red peppers, drained

1 clove garlic, minced

¾ cup reduced-sodium chicken broth, defatted

¾ cup evaporated skimmed milk

¼ cup packed fresh basil leaves

¾ teaspoon salt

¼ teaspoon freshly ground black pepper

1 teaspoon cornstarch

¼ cup grated Parmesan cheese

1. In a large pot of boiling water, cook the pasta until just tender. Add the green beans for the last 2 minutes of cooking time. Drain well.

2. Meanwhile, in a large nonstick skillet, heat 2 teaspoons of the oil until hot but not smoking over medium heat. Add the chicken and cook, stirring, until browned, about 5 minutes. With a slotted spoon, transfer the chicken to a plate.

3. Add the remaining 1 teaspoon oil to the skillet. Add the roasted peppers and garlic and cook, stirring, until the garlic is fragrant, about 1 minute. Stir in the broth, ½ cup of the evaporated milk, the basil, salt, and black pepper and bring to a boil. Reduce to a simmer and cook until slightly thickened, about 3 minutes. Transfer the mixture to a food processor and process to a smooth purée.

4. In a small bowl, combine the remaining ¼ cup evaporated milk with the cornstarch. Return the basil-pepper purée to the skillet along with the chicken and the cornstarch mixture. Bring to a boil over medium heat and cook, stirring, until the sauce is slightly thickened, about 1 minute. Toss the sauce with the hot pasta and green beans. Divide among 4 plates, sprinkle the Parmesan over, and serve.

Helpful hint: You can substitute broccoli for the green beans, if you like.

FAT: 7G/13%
CALORIES: 497
SATURATED FAT: 1.9G
CARBOHYDRATE: 69G
PROTEIN: 36G
CHOLESTEROL: 55MG
SODIUM: 850MG

Boneless chicken breasts are a key ingredient in quick dinners, and when you flatten them slightly and cut them into narrow strips, they cook even faster. For a delightful sweet-and-sour quality, the base for this chicken and vegetable sauce is made from tomatoes accented with vinegar, brown sugar, raisins, and orange zest.

CHICKEN AND BROCCOLI SAUCE

SERVES: 4
WORKING TIME: 35 MINUTES
TOTAL TIME: 35 MINUTES

1 tablespoon olive oil

¾ pound skinless, boneless chicken breasts, lightly pounded (see tip) and cut crosswise into ¼-inch-wide strips

10 ounces medium tube pasta, such as penne rigate, penne, or ziti

1 red onion, sliced

1 red bell pepper, cut into thin strips

2 cloves garlic, minced

3 cups diced plum tomatoes or canned no-salt-added tomatoes, chopped with their juices

1½ cups reduced-sodium chicken broth, defatted

¼ cup golden raisins

½ teaspoon grated orange zest

½ teaspoon salt

¼ teaspoon freshly ground black pepper

4 cups small broccoli florets

1 teaspoon cornstarch

2 teaspoons firmly packed light brown sugar

1 tablespoon balsamic vinegar

1. In a large nonstick skillet, heat 2 teaspoons of the oil until hot but not smoking over medium heat. Add the chicken and cook, stirring, until lightly browned, about 5 minutes. With a slotted spoon, transfer the chicken to a plate.

2. In a large pot of boiling water, cook the pasta until just tender. Drain well.

3. Meanwhile, add the remaining 1 teaspoon oil to the skillet. Add the onion, bell pepper, and garlic and cook, stirring, until the onion begins to soften, about 4 minutes. Add the tomatoes, broth, raisins, orange zest, salt, and black pepper and bring to a boil. Reduce to a simmer and cook until the sauce is slightly reduced, about 5 minutes. Return to a boil and add the broccoli. Reduce to a simmer and cook until the broccoli is tender, about 5 minutes.

4. In a small bowl, combine the cornstarch, brown sugar, and vinegar. Return the chicken to the pan and stir in the cornstarch mixture. Bring to a boil and cook, stirring, until the sauce is slightly thickened and the chicken is heated through, about 1 minute. Toss the sauce with the hot pasta and serve.

Helpful hint: Freezing the chicken breasts for about 15 minutes (after pounding them) will make them easier to cut.

FAT: 6G/10%
CALORIES: 524
SATURATED FAT: 1G
CARBOHYDRATE: 82G
PROTEIN: 37G
CHOLESTEROL: 49MG
SODIUM: 595MG

TIP

Place the chicken breasts between two sheets of plastic wrap or waxed paper and pound the thicker end lightly with a meat pounder or the flat side of small skillet.

GARLIC CHICKEN SAUCE

SERVES: 4
WORKING TIME: 25 MINUTES
TOTAL TIME: 30 MINUTES

Garlic lovers will applaud this assertive sauce laced with pungent slivers of sautéed garlic. The sauce is made with roasted-pepper purée to ensure a thick, "clingy" coating for the pasta strands; anchovy paste lends a savory kick. For a trattoria-style dinner, accompany the pasta with grissini (thin, crisp bread sticks) and follow it with a colorful tossed salad.

10 ounces medium strand pasta, such as linguine, spaghetti, or long fusilli

1 cup jarred roasted red peppers, rinsed and drained

1 tablespoon olive oil

1 onion, finely chopped

6 cloves garlic, slivered

1 red bell pepper, cut into ½-inch squares

¾ pound skinless, boneless chicken breasts, cut into ½-inch chunks

1 cup reduced-sodium chicken broth, defatted

½ cup chopped fresh basil

1 tablespoon anchovy paste, or 2 tablespoons grated Parmesan cheese

1. In a large pot of boiling water, cook the pasta until just tender. Drain well.

2. Meanwhile, in a food processor, process the jarred roasted peppers to a smooth purée; set aside. In a large nonstick skillet, heat the oil until hot but not smoking over medium heat. Add the onion and garlic and cook, stirring frequently, until the onion is softened, about 7 minutes. Add the bell pepper and cook, stirring frequently, until the bell pepper is crisp-tender, about 4 minutes.

3. Add the chicken to the pan and cook until no longer pink, about 2 minutes. Stir the puréed peppers into the skillet along with the broth, basil, and anchovy paste. Simmer until the chicken is just cooked through, about 2 minutes. Toss the sauce with the hot pasta, divide among 4 bowls, and serve.

Helpful hint: Keep a watchful eye on the garlic as it sautés; scorched garlic has an unpleasant, bitter flavor.

FAT: 6G/12%
CALORIES: 452
SATURATED FAT: 1G
CARBOHYDRATE: 65G
PROTEIN: 32G
CHOLESTEROL: 52MG
SODIUM: 442MG

SOUTHWESTERN CHICKEN SAUCE

SERVES: 4
WORKING TIME: 20 MINUTES
TOTAL TIME: 45 MINUTES

1 tablespoon olive oil

½ pound skinless, boneless chicken breasts, cut into ½-inch chunks

1 red bell pepper, diced

1 green bell pepper, diced

1 cup sliced scallions

1 clove garlic, minced

1 teaspoon ground cumin

1½ cups reduced-sodium chicken broth, defatted

10-ounce package frozen corn kernels, thawed

2 cups diced plum tomatoes or canned no-salt-added tomatoes, chopped with their juices

1 teaspoon salt

10 ounces shaped pasta, such as ruote (wagon wheels) or medium shells

1 teaspoon cornstarch

¼ cup reduced-fat sour cream

½ cup diced avocado

½ cup chopped fresh cilantro or basil

1. In a large nonstick skillet, heat 2 teaspoons of the oil until hot but not smoking over medium heat. Add the chicken and cook, stirring, until browned, about 5 minutes. With a slotted spoon, transfer the chicken to a plate.

2. Add the remaining 1 teaspoon oil to the skillet. Add the bell peppers, scallions, and garlic and cook, stirring frequently, until the peppers begin to soften, about 5 minutes. Add the cumin and cook, stirring, until fragrant, about 30 seconds. Add 1¼ cups of the broth, the corn, tomatoes, and salt and bring to a boil. Reduce to a simmer, cover, and cook until the sauce is slightly thickened, about 10 minutes.

3. Meanwhile, in a large pot of boiling water, cook the pasta until just tender. Drain well.

4. In a small bowl, combine the remaining ¼ cup broth and the cornstarch. Stir the cornstarch mixture into the skillet along with the sour cream. Cook, stirring constantly, until the sauce is slightly thickened, about 1 minute. Return the chicken to the pan, stir in the avocado and cilantro, and cook until the chicken is heated through, about 1 minute. Toss the sauce with the hot pasta, divide among 4 bowls, and serve.

Helpful hint: Add a pinch of cayenne pepper (with the cumin in step 2), if you like your pasta sauce spicy.

FAT: 11G/19%
CALORIES: 521
SATURATED FAT: 2.4G
CARBOHYDRATE: 80G
PROTEIN: 29G
CHOLESTEROL: 38MG
SODIUM: 829MG

A Southwestern sauce is the perfect topping for whimsical wagon-wheel pasta. Although the flavors of tomatoes, garlic, cumin, and cilantro may remind you of chili, this dish is not too spicy; on the contrary, the avocado and sour cream bring a particularly mellow quality to the sauce. If you serve a salad with this, garnish the greens with some oven-toasted tortilla triangles.

NEAPOLITAN CHICKEN SAUCE

SERVES: 4
WORKING TIME: 25 MINUTES
TOTAL TIME: 30 MINUTES

Dishes from Naples are typically lavished with robust, garlicky tomato sauce and topped with mozzarella. In fact, the classic pizza is a Neapolitan invention. This bountiful main dish includes both the sauce and the cheese, along with chunks of chicken and Italian sausage. The flavors of garlic and fennel—dominant seasonings in the sausage—suffuse the entire dish.

10 ounces fine strand pasta, such as spaghettini or capellini

3 ounces sweet or hot Italian pork sausage, casings removed

1 cup reduced-sodium chicken broth, defatted

10 ounces skinless, boneless chicken breasts, cut into ½-inch chunks

4 cloves garlic, minced

14½-ounce can no-salt-added stewed tomatoes, chopped with their juices

2 tablespoons no-salt-added tomato paste

½ cup chopped fresh parsley

½ teaspoon freshly ground black pepper

¼ teaspoon salt

1 cup frozen peas, thawed

¾ cup shredded part-skim mozzarella cheese (3 ounces)

1. In a large pot of boiling water, cook the pasta until just tender. Drain well.

2. Meanwhile, crumble the sausage into a large nonstick skillet. Add ¼ cup of the broth and cook over medium heat, stirring, until the sausage is no longer pink, about 4 minutes. Add the chicken and garlic and cook, stirring occasionally, until the chicken is no longer pink, about 4 minutes.

3. Stir the tomatoes, tomato paste, parsley, pepper, salt, and the remaining ¾ cup broth into the pan and bring to a boil. Reduce to a simmer and cook until the chicken is cooked through and the sauce is flavorful, about 3 minutes. Add the peas and cook just until heated through, about 2 minutes. Toss the sauce with the hot pasta, sprinkle the mozzarella over, and serve.

Helpful hints: To prepare the sausage for this recipe, slit the casings lengthwise with the tip of a sharp knife, then peel off the casings with your fingers. If you prefer, use Italian-style turkey sausage instead of pork sausage.

FAT: 12G/20%
CALORIES: 541
SATURATED FAT: 5G
CARBOHYDRATE: 68G
PROTEIN: 38G
CHOLESTEROL: 70MG
SODIUM: 648MG

CHUNKY CHICKEN AND VEGETABLE SAUCE

SERVES: 4
WORKING TIME: 25 MINUTES
TOTAL TIME: 40 MINUTES

With a full complement of hearty vegetables, including potatoes, carrots, parsnips, leek, and garlic, this pasta dish captures the warm and comforting flavors of chicken stew. Rather than pouring in cream to enrich the sauce, however, we've used one of the best fat-cutting tricks around—puréeing some of the cooked vegetables to thicken the broth.

1 tablespoon olive oil

¾ pound skinless, boneless chicken breasts, cut into ½-inch chunks

½ pound red potatoes, cut into ¼-inch dice

2 carrots, cut into ¼-inch dice

2 parsnips, cut into ¼-inch dice

1 cup sliced leek or diced onion

2 cloves garlic, minced

2¾ cups reduced-sodium chicken broth, defatted

¾ teaspoon dried thyme

½ teaspoon salt

¼ teaspoon freshly ground black pepper

10 ounces small tube pasta, such as elbow macaroni or ditalini

1 cup frozen peas, thawed

⅓ cup reduced-fat sour cream

1. In a large nonstick skillet, heat 2 teaspoons of the oil until hot but not smoking over medium heat. Add the chicken and cook, stirring, until browned, about 5 minutes. With a slotted spoon, transfer the chicken to a plate.

2. Add the remaining 1 teaspoon oil to the skillet and add the potatoes, carrots, parsnips, leek, and garlic. Cook, stirring, until the potatoes are lightly browned, about 5 minutes. Add the broth, thyme, salt, and pepper and bring to boil. Reduce the heat to a simmer, cover, and cook until the vegetables are tender and the sauce is slightly thickened, about 15 minutes.

3. Meanwhile, in large pot of boiling water, cook the pasta until just tender. Drain well.

4. Transfer about 1 cup of the vegetable-broth mixture to a food processor or blender and process to a smooth purée. Return the purée and the chicken to the skillet along with the peas and cook until the chicken and peas are heated through, about 2 minutes. Toss the sauce with the hot pasta. Divide among 4 bowls, top with a dollop of the sour cream, and serve.

Helpful hint: Instead of puréeing 1 cup of the soup in a food processor or blender (step 4), you can use a hand blender to purée some of the vegetables right in the skillet.

FAT: 9G/14%
CALORIES: 581
SATURATED FAT: 2.3G
CARBOHYDRATE: 88G
PROTEIN: 37G
CHOLESTEROL: 56MG
SODIUM: 799MG

SPICY SAUSAGE AND BEAN SAUCE

SERVES: 4
WORKING TIME: 20 MINUTES
TOTAL TIME: 45 MINUTES

Though the resemblance may escape American eyes, radiatore pasta was inspired by the shape of an Italian radiator—which makes it a perfect match for a spicy warming sauce! Keep in mind the spicy heat of the main dish and offer cool accompaniments such as a lightly dressed salad and tall, cold drinks.

1 tablespoon olive oil

10 ounces hot Italian-style turkey sausage, casings removed

10 ounces shaped pasta, such as radiatore or rotini

1 red onion, coarsely chopped

1 red bell pepper, diced

2 cloves garlic, minced

2 teaspoons chili powder

28-ounce can no-salt-added tomatoes, chopped with their juices

16-ounce can pinto beans, rinsed and drained

4½-ounce can chopped mild green chilies, drained

½ teaspoon dried oregano

¼ teaspoon freshly ground black pepper

1. In a large nonstick skillet, heat 2 teaspoons of the oil until hot but not smoking over medium heat. Crumble the sausage into the pan and cook, stirring, until cooked through, 6 to 7 minutes. With a slotted spoon, transfer the sausage to a plate.

2. In a large pot of boiling water, cook the pasta until just tender. Drain well.

3. Meanwhile, add the remaining 1 teaspoon oil to the skillet. Add the onion, bell pepper, and garlic and cook, stirring, until the onion begins to soften, 4 to 5 minutes. Add the chili powder and cook until fragrant, about 30 seconds. Return the sausage to the pan and add the tomatoes, beans, green chilies, oregano, and black pepper. Bring the mixture to a boil, reduce to a simmer, cover, and cook until the sauce is slightly thickened, about 15 minutes.

4. Toss the sauce with the hot pasta, divide among 4 bowls, and serve.

Helpful hint: To prepare the sausage for this recipe, slit the casings lengthwise with the tip of a sharp knife, then peel off the casings with your fingers.

FAT: 13G/21%
CALORIES: 551
SATURATED FAT: 2.8G
CARBOHYDRATE: 82G
PROTEIN: 28G
CHOLESTEROL: 38MG
SODIUM: 891MG

CHICKEN AND MUSHROOM SAUCE

SERVES: 4
WORKING TIME: 35 MINUTES
TOTAL TIME: 35 MINUTES

There's subtle sophistication in this unique sauce, perhaps because the mushrooms pick up the delicate bouquet of the white wine and sherry.

10 ounces medium strand pasta, such as long fusilli, linguine, or spaghetti

2 teaspoons olive oil

¼ cup plus 2 tablespoons coarsely chopped pancetta or Canadian bacon (2 ounces)

¾ pound skinless, boneless chicken breasts, cut into ½-inch chunks

1 onion, minced

3 cloves garlic, minced

½ pound mushrooms, thinly sliced

¼ cup dry white wine

3 tablespoons dry sherry

1 cup reduced-sodium chicken broth, defatted

2 tablespoons no-salt-added tomato paste

½ teaspoon salt

½ teaspoon dried rosemary

¼ teaspoon freshly ground black pepper

⅓ cup plus 1 tablespoon chopped fresh parsley

2 tablespoons reduced-fat sour cream

1. In a large pot of boiling water, cook the pasta until just tender. Drain well.

2. Meanwhile, in a large nonstick skillet, heat the oil until hot but not smoking over medium heat. Add the pancetta and cook until slightly crisp, about 3 minutes. Add the chicken and cook, stirring frequently, until lightly browned and cooked through, about 4 minutes. With a slotted spoon, transfer the chicken to a plate.

3. Add the onion and garlic to the pan and cook, stirring frequently, until the onion is softened, about 7 minutes. Add the mushrooms and cook, stirring frequently, until tender, about 4 minutes. Add the wine and sherry, increase the heat to high, and cook until almost evaporated, about 2 minutes.

4. Stir the broth, tomato paste, salt, rosemary, and pepper into the pan and bring to a boil. Reduce the heat to medium, return the chicken to the pan, and cook until heated through, about 1 minute. Remove from the heat, stir in ⅓ cup of the parsley and the sour cream. Toss the sauce with the hot pasta, sprinkle the remaining 1 tablespoon parsley over, and serve.

Helpful hint: You can substitute additional white wine or chicken broth for the sherry, if you like.

FAT: 7G/14%
CALORIES: 466
SATURATED FAT: 1.6G
CARBOHYDRATE: 63G
PROTEIN: 36G
CHOLESTEROL: 59MG
SODIUM: 570MG

CHICKEN PARMIGIANA SAUCE

SERVES: 4
WORKING TIME: 25 MINUTES
TOTAL TIME: 30 MINUTES

10 ounces rigatoni
½ cup grated Parmesan cheese
2 tablespoons flour
¼ teaspoon freshly ground black pepper
10 ounces skinless, boneless chicken breasts, cut crosswise into ½-inch-wide strips
1 tablespoon olive oil
1½ cups canned no-salt-added tomatoes, chopped with their juices
½ cup reduced-sodium chicken broth, defatted
1 tablespoon no-salt-added tomato paste
½ cup chopped fresh basil
¾ teaspoon salt
¼ teaspoon hot pepper sauce

1. In a large pot of boiling water, cook the pasta until just tender. Drain well.

2. Meanwhile, on a sheet of waxed paper, combine 2 tablespoons of the Parmesan, the flour, and pepper. Dredge the chicken in the Parmesan mixture, patting the mixture onto the chicken.

3. In a large nonstick skillet, heat the oil until hot but not smoking over medium heat. Add the chicken and cook, turning the pieces as they brown, until browned all over, about 5 minutes. Add the tomatoes, broth, tomato paste, basil, salt, and hot pepper sauce and bring to a boil. Reduce to a simmer and cook until the sauce is slightly thickened and the chicken is cooked through, about 3 minutes.

4. Toss the sauce with the hot pasta and the remaining 6 tablespoons Parmesan. Divide among 4 bowls and serve.

Helpful hint: Freshly grated Italian Parmesan (which says "Parmigiano-Reggiano" on the rind) will make a big flavor difference in this recipe, and in any recipe calling for Parmesan cheese.

FAT: 9G/18%
CALORIES: 460
SATURATED FAT: 2.8G
CARBOHYDRATE: 62G
PROTEIN: 32G
CHOLESTEROL: 49MG
SODIUM: 743MG

While it's not loaded with cheese (which is high in fat), this pasta sauce is full of potent Parmesan flavor.

SMOKED TURKEY, JACK CHEESE, AND PEPPER SAUCE

SERVES: 4
WORKING TIME: 30 MINUTES
TOTAL TIME: 30 MINUTES

For a memorable macaroni-and-cheese variation, try this lively stovetop casserole. Instead of Cheddar or American cheese, the velvety sauce is rich with melted jalapeño jack. Cubes of smoked turkey and apple, corn kernels, and bell pepper squares give the dish a confetti-like quality. A salad of sliced cucumbers and sweet red onions would offer a pleasant contrast to the pasta.

10 ounces shaped pasta, such as orecchiette or farfalle (bow ties)

1 tablespoon olive oil

4 scallions, thinly sliced

1 red bell pepper, cut into ½-inch squares

1 green bell pepper, cut into ½-inch squares

6 ounces unsliced smoked turkey, cut into ½-inch cubes

1 Granny Smith apple, cored and cut into ½-inch cubes

2 tablespoons flour

2 cups low-fat (1%) milk

¼ teaspoon salt

1 cup frozen corn kernels

1 cup shredded jalapeño jack cheese (4 ounces)

1. In a large pot of boiling water, cook the pasta until just tender. Drain well.

2. Meanwhile, in a large nonstick skillet, heat the oil until hot but not smoking over medium heat. Add the scallions and cook until softened, about 2 minutes. Add the bell peppers and cook, stirring frequently, until crisp-tender, about 4 minutes.

3. Add the turkey and apple to the pan and cook, stirring frequently, until the apple is crisp-tender, about 3 minutes. Stir in the flour until well combined. Gradually add the milk. Stir in the salt and cook, stirring constantly, until the sauce is slightly thickened and no floury taste remains, about 5 minutes. Add the corn and cheese and cook just until the corn is heated through and the cheese is melted, about 2 minutes. Toss the sauce with the hot pasta and serve.

Helpful hint: For a milder meal, substitute regular Monterey jack cheese for the jalapeño jack (the latter is studded with bits of chili pepper).

FAT: 17G/26%
CALORIES: 588
SATURATED FAT: 7G
CARBOHYDRATE: 81G
PROTEIN: 31G
CHOLESTEROL: 57MG
SODIUM: 826MG

SWEET AND SAVORY GROUND TURKEY SAUCE

SERVES: 4
WORKING TIME: 25 MINUTES
TOTAL TIME: 35 MINUTES

Turkey's light flavor is perfect for this intriguingly tangy "meat" sauce. For the healthiest meal, be sure to get lean ground turkey—skinless breast meat only—or cut up a piece of turkey breast and grind it yourself in the food processor. Chili sauce and Dijon mustard do their bit for the spicy side, while honey and orange juice balance things out with sweet and tart notes.

10 ounces medium tube pasta, such as ziti or penne

1 tablespoon olive oil

4 scallions, thinly sliced

3 cloves garlic, minced

1 green bell pepper, cut into ½-inch squares

1 carrot, quartered lengthwise and thinly sliced

10 ounces lean ground turkey

14½-ounce can no-salt-added stewed tomatoes

½ cup reduced-sodium chicken broth, defatted

¼ cup orange juice

¼ cup chili sauce

1 tablespoon Dijon mustard

1 tablespoon honey

½ teaspoon dried sage

½ teaspoon salt

½ teaspoon freshly ground black pepper

1 teaspoon cornstarch mixed with 1 tablespoon water

1. In a large pot of boiling water, cook the pasta until just tender. Drain well.

2. Meanwhile, in a large nonstick skillet, heat the oil until hot but not smoking over medium heat. Add the scallions and garlic and cook, stirring, until the scallions are softened, about 2 minutes. Add the bell pepper and carrot and cook, stirring frequently, until the pepper and carrot are softened, about 5 minutes. Crumble in the turkey and cook until no longer pink, about 4 minutes.

3. Add the tomatoes, broth, orange juice, chili sauce, mustard, honey, sage, salt, and black pepper to the pan and bring to a boil. Reduce to a simmer, cover, and cook until the sauce is richly flavored, about 5 minutes. Return to a boil, stir in the cornstarch mixture, and cook, stirring constantly, until the sauce is slightly thickened, about 1 minute. Toss the sauce with the hot pasta, divide among 4 bowls, and serve.

Helpful hint: You can make the sauce a day ahead; its flavors will blend and mellow with time. Reheat it over medium-low heat, adding a little chicken broth or water if it is too thick.

FAT: 10G/18%
CALORIES: 491
SATURATED FAT: 2G
CARBOHYDRATE: 76G
PROTEIN: 24G
CHOLESTEROL: 52MG
SODIUM: 761MG

Mixing sweet spices (like cinnamon, nutmeg, and cloves) with savory flavors (like onion, peppers, and garlic) has a long culinary history in Italy. This Italian-inspired sauce is made with ground turkey and spiked with orange zest, fennel seeds, and a number of sweet and savory spices.

TURKEY SAUCE WITH ORANGE AND SWEET SPICES

SERVES: 4
WORKING TIME: 20 MINUTES
TOTAL TIME: 40 MINUTES

1 tablespoon olive oil

1 onion, diced

2 cloves garlic, minced

¾ pound lean ground turkey

1 teaspoon fennel seeds, crushed (see tip)

¾ teaspoon grated orange zest

½ teaspoon cinnamon

⅛ teaspoon nutmeg

⅛ teaspoon ground cloves

⅛ teaspoon cayenne pepper

2 cups diced fresh fennel or celery

1 red bell pepper, diced

2¼ cups reduced-sodium chicken broth, defatted

3 tablespoons no-salt-added tomato paste

1 tablespoon honey

½ teaspoon salt

10 ounces medium strand pasta, such as spaghetti or linguine

1 tablespoon red wine vinegar

1. In a large nonstick skillet, heat the oil until hot but not smoking over medium heat. Add the onion and garlic and cook, stirring, until the onion begins to soften, 3 to 4 minutes. Crumble in the turkey and cook until no longer pink, about 5 minutes. Stir in the fennel seeds, orange zest, cinnamon, nutmeg, cloves, and cayenne and cook until fragrant, about 1 minute.

2. Stir the fresh fennel, bell pepper, broth, tomato paste, honey, and salt into the pan and bring to a boil. Reduce to a simmer, cover, and cook until the sauce is richly flavored and thickened, about 20 minutes.

3. Meanwhile, in a large pot of boiling water, cook the pasta until just tender. Drain well.

4. Add the vinegar to the sauce and stir to combine. Toss the sauce with the hot pasta, divide among 4 bowls, and serve.

Helpful hint: If you like, you can substitute another type of vinegar—such as white wine or cider—for the red wine vinegar.

FAT: 11G/20%
CALORIES: 485
SATURATED FAT: 2.3G
CARBOHYDRATE: 67G
PROTEIN: 28G
CHOLESTEROL: 62MG
SODIUM: 739MG

TIP

Although fennel can be purchased already ground, its flavor will be more intense if you buy the seeds and crush them with a mortar and pestle—the traditional kitchen tool for grinding spices at home. This set is marble; porcelain mortar-and-pestle sets, in a variety of sizes, are also widely available. You can use a mortar and pestle for other whole spices too—cumin, cloves, coriander, anise, and the like.

CHICKEN ARRABBIATA SAUCE

SERVES: 4
WORKING TIME: 30 MINUTES
TOTAL TIME: 40 MINUTES

The Italian word "arrabbiata" means "furious" and refers here to the peppery heat of the sauce. Whole chicken breasts are traditionally cooked in this type of sauce, but we've used chunks of chicken instead, along with rigatoni. For dessert, serve palate-cooling portions of Italian lemon or orange ice with fresh fruit.

1 tablespoon olive oil

¾ pound skinless, boneless, chicken breasts, cut into ½-inch chunks

10 ounces rigatoni

1 onion, diced

2 cloves garlic, minced

28-ounce can tomatoes in purée

1 tablespoon minced fresh ginger

¾ teaspoon dried rosemary

½ teaspoon salt

¼ teaspoon red pepper flakes

2 tablespoons capers, rinsed and drained

1 tablespoon balsamic vinegar

1. In a large nonstick skillet, heat 2 teaspoons of the oil until hot but not smoking over medium heat. Add the chicken and cook, stirring, until browned, about 5 minutes. With a slotted spoon, transfer the chicken to a plate.

2. In a large pot of boiling water, cook the pasta until just tender. Drain well.

3. Meanwhile, add the remaining 1 teaspoon oil to the skillet. Add the onion and garlic and cook, stirring, until the onion is softened, about 4 minutes. Stir in the tomatoes, ginger, rosemary, salt, and red pepper flakes. Cover and cook until the sauce is richly flavored and slightly thickened, 10 to 12 minutes.

4. Return the chicken to the pan along with the capers and vinegar and cook until the chicken is heated through, about 1 minute. Toss the sauce with the hot pasta, divide among 4 plates, and serve.

Helpful hint: Red pepper flakes are small bits of dried hot red chili peppers. Start with a tiny pinch and add more gradually if you don't want too "furious" a sauce.

FAT: 6G/12%
CALORIES: 460
SATURATED FAT: 0.9G
CARBOHYDRATE: 70G
PROTEIN: 31G
CHOLESTEROL: 49MG
SODIUM: 761MG

Lemon Chicken Sauce

SERVES: 4
WORKING TIME: 30 MINUTES
TOTAL TIME: 30 MINUTES

10 ounces medium strand pasta, such as perciatelli, linguine, or spaghetti

2 teaspoons olive oil

3 shallots or scallions, finely chopped

1 clove garlic, minced

¾ pound skinless, boneless chicken thighs, cut into ½-inch chunks

½ teaspoon salt

½ teaspoon ground ginger

¼ teaspoon freshly ground black pepper

1 cup reduced-sodium chicken broth, defatted

1 teaspoon grated lemon zest

3 tablespoons fresh lemon juice

⅓ cup snipped fresh dill

1 cup frozen peas

2 tablespoons reduced-fat cream cheese (Neufchâtel)

1½ teaspoons cornstarch mixed with 1 tablespoon water

1. In a large pot of boiling water, cook the pasta until just tender. Drain well.

2. Meanwhile, in a large nonstick skillet, heat the oil until hot but not smoking over medium heat. Add the shallots and garlic and cook, stirring frequently, until the shallots are tender, about 2 minutes. Add the chicken, sprinkle with the salt, ginger, and pepper, and cook, stirring frequently, until the chicken is no longer pink, about 3 minutes.

3. Stir the broth, lemon zest, lemon juice, and dill into the pan and bring to a boil. Reduce to a simmer and cook until the chicken is cooked through, about 2 minutes. Stir in the peas and cream cheese and cook just until the peas are heated through and the cream cheese is melted, about 2 minutes. Stir in the cornstarch mixture and cook, stirring, until the sauce is slightly thickened, about 1 minute. Toss the sauce with the hot pasta, divide among 4 bowls, and serve.

Helpful hint: Be sure to grate the lemon zest before squeezing the lemon. Any extra lemon zest can be frozen for future use.

Lemon, dill, and green peas, used together in a single dish, carry an unmistakable suggestion of spring. And a delicate sauce made with reduced-fat cream cheese keeps this dish light. Any sort of long pasta would work with this sauce; perciatelli (shown here) looks like thick spaghetti but the strands are actually hollow in the middle.

FAT: 8G/16%
CALORIES: 450
SATURATED FAT: 2.2G
CARBOHYDRATE: 63G
PROTEIN: 30G
CHOLESTEROL: 74MG
SODIUM: 573MG

CURRIED CHICKEN SAUCE

SERVES: 4
WORKING TIME: 30 MINUTES
TOTAL TIME: 30 MINUTES

The sunstruck colors of this inventive dish are matched by its vibrant flavor. The unconventional pairing of curry sauce and pasta may startle traditionalists, but just persuade them to sample a forkful of this warmly seasoned cream sauce with flavorful vegetables and they'll willingly forgo tradition for once.

10 ounces shaped pasta, such as farfalle (bow ties) or orecchiette

1 tablespoon olive oil

2 scallions, thinly sliced

1 red bell pepper, cut into ½-inch squares

1 green bell pepper, cut into ½-inch squares

2 carrots, halved lengthwise and thinly sliced

¾ pound skinless, boneless chicken breasts, cut into ½-inch chunks

1 cup reduced-sodium chicken broth, defatted

¾ cup plain nonfat yogurt

3 tablespoons reduced-fat sour cream

2 tablespoons flour

1 tablespoon no-salt-added tomato paste

2 teaspoons curry powder

½ teaspoon ground ginger

1. In a large pot of boiling water, cook the pasta until just tender. Drain well.

2. Meanwhile, in a large nonstick skillet, heat the oil until hot but not smoking over medium heat. Add the scallions, bell peppers, and carrots and cook, stirring frequently, until the carrots are crisp-tender, about 5 minutes. Add the chicken and cook until no longer pink, about 2 minutes. Add the broth and bring to a boil. Reduce to a simmer.

3. Meanwhile, in a small bowl, combine the yogurt, sour cream, flour, tomato paste, curry powder, and ginger. Stir the yogurt mixture into the simmering broth and cook, stirring constantly, until slightly thickened and no floury taste remains, about 3 minutes. Toss the sauce with the hot pasta and serve.

Helpful hint: Combining the yogurt and sour cream with flour keeps the dairy products from curdling when the mixture is added to the simmering broth. Still, you should be careful not to bring the mixture to a boil after adding the yogurt mixture.

FAT: 7G/13%
CALORIES: 482
SATURATED FAT: 1.7G
CARBOHYDRATE: 68G
PROTEIN: 34G
CHOLESTEROL: 54MG
SODIUM: 257MG

Ragù of Chicken

SERVES: 4
WORKING TIME: 25 MINUTES
TOTAL TIME: 40 MINUTES

Ragù, as it is made in Bologna, is a rich meat sauce finished with a spoonful of cream. Here's a lighter version to enjoy.

1 tablespoon olive oil

6 tablespoons finely diced Canadian bacon (2 ounces)

¾ pound ground chicken

10 ounces medium strand pasta, such as linguine or spaghetti

1 onion, diced

2 carrots, diced

2 ribs celery, diced

1 clove garlic, minced

¼ cup Marsala wine or dry red wine

28-ounce can no-salt-added crushed tomatoes

½ teaspoon dried oregano

½ teaspoon dried thyme

½ teaspoon salt

2 teaspoons flour

½ cup low-fat (1%) milk

1. In a large nonstick skillet, heat 2 teaspoons of the oil until hot but not smoking over medium heat. Add the Canadian bacon and cook, stirring, until the bacon is browned, about 2 minutes. Add the chicken and cook, stirring to break up the meat, until the chicken is cooked through, about 5 minutes. With a slotted spoon, transfer the chicken and bacon to a plate.

2. In a large pot of boiling water, cook the pasta until just tender. Drain well.

3. Meanwhile, add the remaining 1 teaspoon oil to the skillet and add the onion, carrots, celery, and garlic. Cook, stirring, until the onion begins to soften, about 4 minutes. Return the chicken and bacon to the skillet along with the Marsala and cook until the Marsala is almost evaporated, about 1 minute. Stir in the tomatoes, oregano, thyme, and salt and bring to boil. Reduce the heat to a simmer, cover, and cook until richly flavored, about 12 minutes.

4. In a small bowl, combine the flour and milk. Stir the milk mixture into the skillet and cook, stirring constantly, until the sauce is slightly thickened, about 1 minute. Toss the sauce with the hot pasta, divide among 4 bowls, and serve.

FAT: 14G/23%
CALORIES: 548
SATURATED FAT: 3.1G
CARBOHYDRATE: 74G
PROTEIN: 31G
CHOLESTEROL: 79MG
SODIUM: 621MG

MEAT SAUCES
2

SOUTHWESTERN CHILI SAUCE

SERVES: 4
WORKING TIME: 30 MINUTES
TOTAL TIME: 30 MINUTES

This hearty pork-and-bean sauce is based on traditional chili, but it's served over pasta for a healthier, high-carbohydrate meal. Tenderloin is the leanest pork cut, and there's no waste whatsoever. And because the meat is cut into small pieces, it cooks in minutes. Serve a green salad dressed with a lime-juice vinaigrette alongside.

10 ounces medium tube pasta, such as penne or ziti

1 tablespoon olive oil

1 onion, finely chopped

3 cloves garlic, minced

1 green bell pepper, cut into ½-inch squares

½ pound well-trimmed pork tenderloin, cut into ½-inch chunks

2 teaspoons chili powder

1 teaspoon ground cumin

½ cup reduced-sodium chicken broth, defatted

8-ounce can no-salt-added tomato sauce

16-ounce can black beans, rinsed and drained

1 pickled jalapeño, seeded and finely chopped

3 tablespoons reduced-fat sour cream

1. In a large pot of boiling water, cook the pasta until just tender. Drain well.

2. Meanwhile, in a large nonstick skillet, heat the oil until hot but not smoking over medium heat. Add the onion and garlic and cook, stirring frequently, until the onion is lightly browned, about 5 minutes. Add the bell pepper and cook, stirring frequently, until the pepper is crisp-tender, about 4 minutes.

3. Add the pork to the pan, sprinkle with the chili powder and cumin, and cook, stirring frequently, until the pork is almost cooked through, about 4 minutes. Stir in the broth and tomato sauce and bring to a boil. Add the beans and the jalapeño and cook until heated through, about 3 minutes. Toss with the hot pasta. Divide among 4 bowls, top with a dollop of the sour cream, and serve.

Helpful hints: As always, when using chili powder, take your family's tastes into consideration. If they don't appreciate hot food, use less chili powder than the recipe calls for. Also, check the label on the jar of chili powder you are using; some chili powders are hot while others are mild. The hot variety is often labeled "Hot Mexican Chili Powder."

FAT: 9G/16%
CALORIES: 495
SATURATED FAT: 2.1G
CARBOHYDRATE: 75G
PROTEIN: 28G
CHOLESTEROL: 41MG
SODIUM: 375MG

Naples
is the home of
pizzaiola sauce, a
simple tomato sauce of
the sort used on pizza.
This particular version
is seasoned with basil
rather than the usual
oregano. The strips of
beef and red bell
pepper harmonize
nicely with long pasta
strands. Although we
call for long fusilli,
any strand pasta will
work well. For a burst
of color, try the sauce
with spinach linguine.

Beef Pizzaiola Sauce

Serves: 4
Working time: 35 minutes
Total time: 35 minutes

10 ounces medium strand pasta, such as long fusilli, linguine, or spaghetti

2 tablespoons flour

½ teaspoon salt

½ pound well-trimmed sirloin, cut into 2 x ¼-inch strips (see tip)

1 tablespoon olive oil

1 onion, halved and thinly sliced

1 red bell pepper, cut into ¼-inch-wide strips

Half of a 10-ounce package Italian flat green beans, thawed and halved crosswise

4 cloves garlic, minced

½ pound plum tomatoes, coarsely chopped

8-ounce can no-salt-added tomato sauce

½ cup chopped fresh basil

1. In a large pot of boiling water, cook the pasta until just tender. Drain well.

2. Meanwhile, on a sheet of waxed paper, combine the flour and salt. Dredge the beef in the flour mixture, shaking off and reserving the excess. In a large nonstick skillet, heat the oil until hot but not smoking over medium heat. Add the beef and cook, stirring frequently, until lightly browned, about 2 minutes.

3. Add the onion, bell pepper, green beans, and garlic to the pan and cook, stirring frequently, until the pepper is tender, about 5 minutes. Sprinkle the reserved flour mixture over, stirring to coat. Add the tomatoes, tomato sauce, and basil and cook until the sauce is slightly thickened, about 4 minutes. Toss with the hot pasta, divide among 4 plates, and serve.

Helpful hint: If you can't get Italian flat green beans, use regular frozen green beans.

Fat: 8g/16%
Calories: 458
Saturated Fat: 1.5g
Carbohydrate: 73g
Protein: 25g
Cholesterol: 35mg
Sodium: 332mg

TIP

To cut the meat, first chill the steak in the freezer for about 15 minutes to firm it. Then, with a long, sharp knife, cut the steak in half horizontally, using a careful sawing motion. Separate the two pieces of meat and cut each piece crosswise into 2 x ¼-inch strips.

PORK PICCATA SAUCE

SERVES: 4
WORKING TIME: 30 MINUTES
TOTAL TIME: 30 MINUTES

10 ounces shaped pasta, such as gemelli, rotini, or radiatore

2 tablespoons flour

½ teaspoon salt

¼ teaspoon freshly ground black pepper

10 ounces well-trimmed pork tenderloin, cut into 2 x ½-inch strips

1 tablespoon olive oil

1 red onion, finely chopped

6 cloves garlic, minced

1 cup reduced-sodium chicken broth, defatted

1 teaspoon grated lemon zest

2 tablespoons fresh lemon juice

¼ cup pimiento-stuffed green olives, coarsely chopped

1 tablespoon capers, rinsed and drained

¼ cup chopped fresh parsley

1. In a large pot of boiling water, cook the pasta until just tender. Drain well.

2. Meanwhile, on a sheet of waxed paper, combine the flour, salt, and pepper. Dredge the pork in the flour mixture, shaking off and reserving the excess. In a large nonstick skillet, heat the oil until hot but not smoking over medium heat. Add the pork and cook, stirring frequently, until lightly browned, about 2 minutes. Add the onion and garlic and cook, stirring frequently, until the onion is crisp-tender, about 5 minutes. Sprinkle the reserved flour over, stirring to combine.

3. Gradually add the broth to the pan, stirring constantly, until well combined. Add the lemon zest, lemon juice, olives, and capers. Cook, stirring constantly, until the sauce is slightly thickened, about 3 minutes. Add the parsley, toss with the hot pasta, divide among 4 plates, and serve.

Helpful hint: If you squeeze a large lemon, you're likely to get more juice than the 2 tablespoons called for here. Use the extra juice in a salad dressing to serve with this meal, or add it to orange or grape juice for an extra-refreshing beverage.

Veal piccata, a fixture on Italian restaurant menus, can also be made with thin cuts of poultry or pork. We've cut the pork tenderloin in strips so it can be tossed with pasta; the familiar lemon-garlic sauce remains the same. Gemelli—the word means "twins"—are double pasta tubes, twisted or scrolled together.

FAT: 8G/17%
CALORIES: 433
SATURATED FAT: 1.6G
CARBOHYDRATE: 63G
PROTEIN: 26G
CHOLESTEROL: 46MG
SODIUM: 720MG

CURRIED LAMB SAUCE

SERVES: 4
WORKING TIME: 20 MINUTES
TOTAL TIME: 30 MINUTES

Lamb and curry are a classic combination; the richness of the meat and the complex spicing of the seasoning are a natural match. Tangy morsels of dried apricot add interest to this short-cut curry, which is served over fettuccine rather than the traditional rice. As a common sense time-saver, the potatoes and pasta are cooked—one after the other—in a single pot.

½ pound all-purpose potatoes, peeled and cut into ½-inch cubes

10 ounces fettuccine

½ pound well-trimmed boneless lamb shoulder, cut into large chunks

2 teaspoons olive oil

4 scallions, thinly sliced

3 cloves garlic, minced

2 teaspoons curry powder

1 teaspoon ground ginger

1 teaspoon salt

Two 8-ounce cans no-salt-added tomato sauce

½ cup dried apricots, coarsely chopped

1 cup frozen peas

1. In a large pot of boiling water, cook the potatoes until firm-tender, about 4 minutes. With a slotted spoon or sieve, transfer the potatoes to a bowl and set aside. In the same pot, cook the pasta until just tender. Drain well.

2. Meanwhile, in a food processor, process the lamb until finely ground, about 30 seconds. In a large nonstick skillet, heat the oil until hot but not smoking over medium heat. Add the scallions and garlic and cook, stirring frequently, until the scallions are tender, about 2 minutes. Add the lamb and cook, stirring frequently, until no longer pink, about 2 minutes. Add the curry powder, ginger, and salt, stirring to coat.

3. Stir the tomato sauce, apricots, and ½ cup of water into the pan and bring to a boil. Reduce to a simmer, add the potatoes, cover, and cook until the sauce is flavorful, about 4 minutes. Add the peas and cook until just heated through. Toss with the hot pasta, divide among 4 plates, and serve.

Helpful hint: After removing the potatoes, be sure the water is still at a rolling boil before adding the pasta (otherwise the strands of fettuccine may stick together).

FAT: 10G/17%
CALORIES: 525
SATURATED FAT: 2.3G
CARBOHYDRATE: 84G
PROTEIN: 26G
CHOLESTEROL: 105MG
SODIUM: 677MG

Lamb and White Bean Sauce

SERVES: 4
WORKING TIME: 25 MINUTES
TOTAL TIME: 25 MINUTES

With their natural meatiness, beans can double the heartiness of any pasta sauce. Here, we've used cannellini (white kidney beans), along with cubes of lamb. Some of the beans are mashed as they cook, so that they thicken the sauce with their starch. The seasonings include dried tarragon and rosemary, as well as a last-minute toss of fresh parsley for a bright green note.

10 ounces medium tube pasta, such as cavatappi, ziti, or penne

2 teaspoons olive oil

½ pound well-trimmed boneless lamb shoulder, cut into ½-inch cubes

6 scallions, thinly sliced

3 cloves garlic, minced

¾ teaspoon dried tarragon

½ teaspoon dried rosemary, crumbled

½ teaspoon salt

1 cup reduced-sodium chicken broth, defatted

2 tablespoons no-salt-added tomato paste

1 cup canned white kidney beans (cannellini), rinsed and drained

¼ cup chopped fresh parsley

1. In a large pot of boiling water, cook the pasta until just tender. Drain well.

2. Meanwhile, in a large nonstick skillet, heat the oil until hot but not smoking over medium heat. Add the lamb and cook, stirring frequently, until no longer pink, about 3 minutes. Add the scallions, garlic, tarragon, rosemary, and salt and cook, stirring frequently, until the scallions are tender, about 3 minutes.

3. Add the broth, tomato paste, and beans to the pan and bring to a boil. Reduce to a simmer and cook, stirring frequently and mashing some of the beans against the side of the skillet, until the sauce is slightly thickened, about 5 minutes. Add the parsley, toss with the hot pasta, and serve.

Helpful hint: Cavatappi, shown here, are hollow ridged pasta twists. The literal translation of the name is "corkscrews." You're more likely to find cavatappi in an imported brand of pasta than a domestic one.

FAT: 8G/16%
CALORIES: 438
SATURATED FAT: 1.9G
CARBOHYDRATE: 65G
PROTEIN: 26G
CHOLESTEROL: 38MG
SODIUM: 556MG

GROUND PORK SAUCE WITH ALMONDS

SERVES: 4
WORKING TIME: 35 MINUTES
TOTAL TIME: 35 MINUTES

The trio of green olives, golden raisins, and sliced almonds lends special interest to this lightly creamy, garlic-scented meat sauce.

10 ounces fettuccine

10 ounces well-trimmed pork tenderloin, cut into chunks

¼ cup evaporated skimmed or low-fat milk

1 tablespoon olive oil

1 red onion, finely chopped

4 cloves garlic, minced

½ cup dry red wine

14½-ounce can no-salt-added stewed tomatoes, chopped with their juices

¼ cup no-salt-added tomato paste

¼ cup golden raisins

¼ cup pimiento-stuffed green olives, coarsely chopped

½ teaspoon dried rosemary, crumbled

½ teaspoon salt

2 tablespoons sliced almonds

1. In a large pot of boiling water, cook the pasta until just tender. Drain well.

2. Meanwhile, in a food processor, process the pork and evaporated milk until the pork is finely ground. In a large nonstick skillet, heat the oil until hot but not smoking over medium heat. Add the onion and garlic and cook, stirring frequently, until the onion is softened, about 7 minutes. Add the pork mixture and cook, stirring frequently, until the pork is no longer pink, about 4 minutes.

3. Add the wine to the pan and cook, stirring frequently, until almost evaporated, about 3 minutes. Stir in the tomatoes, the tomato paste, raisins, olives, rosemary, and salt. Simmer, stirring frequently, until the sauce is thickened and richly flavored, about 5 minutes. Stir in the almonds and toss with the hot pasta. Divide among 4 plates and serve.

Helpful hint: Although we call for golden raisins, dark raisins would be fine in this recipe.

FAT: 12G/21%
CALORIES: 517
SATURATED FAT: 2.2G
CARBOHYDRATE: 75G
PROTEIN: 30G
CHOLESTEROL: 114MG
SODIUM: 583MG

LENTIL AND SAUSAGE SAUCE

SERVES: 4
WORKING TIME: 20 MINUTES
TOTAL TIME: 55 MINUTES

2 teaspoons olive oil

3 ounces Spanish-style chorizo, or pepperoni, coarsely chopped

1 onion, finely chopped

1 green bell pepper, finely chopped

2 carrots, finely diced

1 cup lentils, rinsed and picked over

2 cups reduced-sodium chicken broth, defatted

½ teaspoon fennel seeds, crushed

½ teaspoon freshly ground black pepper

10 ounces shaped pasta, such as gnocchi, radiatore, or ruote (wagon wheels)

3 tablespoons reduced-fat sour cream

4 teaspoons flour

1. In a large nonstick skillet, heat the oil until hot but not smoking over medium heat. Add the chorizo and cook, stirring frequently, until lightly crisped, about 2 minutes. Add the onion and cook, stirring frequently, until the onion is softened, about 5 minutes.

2. Add the bell pepper and carrots to the pan, stirring for 1 minute to coat. Add the lentils, stirring to combine. Add the broth, 2 cups of water, the fennel, and black pepper and bring to a boil. Reduce to a simmer, cover, and cook until the lentils are very tender, about 35 minutes.

3. Meanwhile, in a large pot of boiling water, cook the pasta until just tender. Drain well.

4. In a small bowl, combine the sour cream and flour. Stir the sour cream mixture into the sauce and cook, stirring, until rich and creamy, about 3 minutes. Toss the sauce with the hot pasta, divide among 4 plates, and serve.

Helpful hint: There is also a Mexican sausage called chorizo, but it differs from the Spanish type used here in that it is made from raw, rather than smoked, pork. If you can't find firm Spanish-style chorizo, use pepperoni instead.

FAT: 15G/22%
CALORIES: 625
SATURATED FAT: 4.7G
CARBOHYDRATE: 93G
PROTEIN: 31G
CHOLESTEROL: 21MG
SODIUM: 745MG

Add pasta to the classic Italian duo of lentils and sausage and the result is a delicious, healthy dish.

PAPRIKASH SAUCE

SERVES: 4
WORKING TIME: 35 MINUTES
TOTAL TIME: 35 MINUTES

Paprika is one of the defining ingredients of Hungarian cuisine. Dishes called "paprikash" (which may be made with poultry, meat, or fish) are lavished with a velvety paprika sauce made with sour cream. Such dishes are traditionally served over dumplings, rice, or egg noodles. Offer a green salad or a steamed green vegetable on the side.

10 ounces wide egg noodles

2 teaspoons olive oil

4 scallions, thinly sliced

3 cloves garlic, minced

½ pound mushrooms, thinly sliced

1 cup jarred roasted red peppers, rinsed and drained

2 tablespoons no-salt-added tomato paste

2 teaspoons paprika

10 ounces well-trimmed top round of beef, cut into chunks

½ cup plain nonfat yogurt

3 tablespoons reduced-fat sour cream

2 tablespoons flour

¾ teaspoon salt

1. In a large pot of boiling water, cook the pasta until just tender. Drain well.

2. Meanwhile, in a large nonstick skillet, heat the oil until hot but not smoking over medium heat. Add the scallions and garlic and cook, stirring frequently, until the scallions are tender, about 2 minutes. Add the mushrooms and cook, stirring frequently, until the mushrooms are slightly softened, about 5 minutes.

3. In a food processor, combine the roasted red peppers, tomato paste, and paprika and process to a smooth purée. Transfer the purée to a small bowl and set aside. In the same processor bowl, process the beef until coarsely chopped.

4. Crumble the ground beef into the skillet and cook until no longer pink, about 4 minutes. Add the pepper purée and cook until the sauce is heated through, about 3 minutes. In a small bowl, combine the yogurt, sour cream, flour, and salt. Stir the yogurt mixture and ⅓ cup of water into the skillet and cook, stirring constantly, until the sauce is slightly thickened and no floury taste remains, about 2 minutes. Toss with the hot pasta, divide among 4 plates, and serve.

Helpful hint: Stirring flour into the yogurt-sour cream mixture helps keep the sauce from "breaking." Stirring gently (not vigorously) helps, too.

FAT: 10G/19%
CALORIES: 473
SATURATED FAT: 2.6G
CARBOHYDRATE: 65G
PROTEIN: 31G
CHOLESTEROL: 112MG
SODIUM: 574MG

*T*he
food processor does
most of the work here,
chopping the beef and
simultaneously
combining it with
cream cheese and
seasonings. After just a
few minutes of
cooking, you have a
beautifully creamy
sauce. As an
accompaniment, brush
whole-grain Italian
bread with a mixture
of olive oil, garlic, and
parsley and toast it
under the broiler.

CREAMED SPINACH SAUCE WITH GROUND BEEF

SERVES: 4
WORKING TIME: 30 MINUTES
TOTAL TIME: 30 MINUTES

10 ounces medium tube pasta, such as penne or ziti

½ pound well-trimmed top round of beef, cut into chunks

1 tablespoon reduced-fat cream cheese (Neufchâtel)

2 teaspoons paprika

½ teaspoon salt

⅛ teaspoon ground allspice

1 tablespoon olive oil

2 onions, finely chopped

4 cloves garlic, minced

2 tablespoons flour

1½ cups low-fat (1%) milk

10-ounce package frozen chopped spinach, thawed and squeezed dry (see tip)

¼ cup grated Parmesan cheese

1. In a large pot of boiling water, cook the pasta until just tender. Drain well.

2. Meanwhile, in a food processor, combine the beef, cream cheese, paprika, salt, and allspice and process until finely chopped. In a large nonstick skillet, heat the oil until hot but not smoking over medium heat. Add the onions and garlic and cook, stirring frequently, until the onions are golden brown, about 5 minutes. Add the beef mixture to the skillet and cook, stirring frequently, until the beef is no longer pink, about 4 minutes.

3. Sprinkle the flour over the beef mixture, stirring, until well combined. Gradually add the milk and cook, stirring frequently, until slightly thickened, about 4 minutes. Add the spinach and cook, stirring frequently, until the spinach is heated through and the sauce is well blended, about 3 minutes. Add the Parmesan and stir to combine. Divide the pasta among 4 plates, spoon the sauce over, and serve.

Helpful hint: To thaw the spinach in the microwave, remove all of the packaging, place the frozen spinach in a microwave-safe container, and microwave on high power for 2 to 3 minutes.

TIP

To prepare frozen spinach, thaw according to package directions, and then squeeze out excess liquid (this keeps the sauce from becoming watery). Work over a bowl as you squeeze the spinach, one handful at a time.

FAT: 10G/18%
CALORIES: 506
SATURATED FAT: 3.3G
CARBOHYDRATE: 73G
PROTEIN: 31G
CHOLESTEROL: 42MG
SODIUM: 522MG

PORK AND BEAN SAUCE

SERVES: 4
WORKING TIME: 35 MINUTES
TOTAL TIME: 35 MINUTES

10 ounces shaped pasta, such as fusilli bucati, rotini, or radiatore

3 tablespoons flour

½ teaspoon salt

¼ teaspoon freshly ground black pepper

½ pound well-trimmed pork tenderloin, cut into ½-inch cubes

2 teaspoons olive oil

3 tablespoons coarsely chopped Canadian bacon (1 ounce)

1 onion, finely chopped

1 green bell pepper, cut into ½-inch squares

Two 8-ounce cans no-salt-added tomato sauce

2 tablespoons firmly packed light brown sugar

1 teaspoon grated orange zest

¼ cup orange juice

10-ounce can pinto beans, rinsed and drained

1. In a large pot of boiling water, cook the pasta until just tender. Drain well.

2. Meanwhile, on a sheet of waxed paper, combine the flour, salt, and black pepper. Dredge the pork in the flour mixture, shaking off and reserving the excess.

3. In a large nonstick skillet, heat the oil until hot but not smoking over medium heat. Add the Canadian bacon and cook until lightly crisped, about 2 minutes. Add the pork and cook, stirring, until the pork is no longer pink, about 4 minutes. Stir in the onion and bell pepper and cook, stirring frequently, until the onion is crisp-tender, about 5 minutes.

4. Sprinkle the reserved flour mixture into the skillet and stir until well coated. Add the tomato sauce, brown sugar, orange zest, and orange juice and bring to a boil. Reduce to a simmer, stir in the beans, and cook until the sauce is slightly thickened, the beans are heated through, and no floury taste remains, about 2 minutes. Toss the sauce with the hot pasta, divide among 4 bowls, and serve.

Helpful hint: The thick pasta twists shown here are fusilli bucati, which are hollow in the middle. Regular rotini would work just as well.

FAT: 7G/12%
CALORIES: 517
SATURATED FAT: 1.3G
CARBOHYDRATE: 86G
PROTEIN: 28G
CHOLESTEROL: 40MG
SODIUM: 550MG

Two kinds of pork—both used in sensible quantities for a low-fat dish—make for a highly flavorful, satisfying pasta sauce. Freshly ground lean pork tenderloin is the real "meat" of the dish, while bits of Canadian bacon bring a smoky savor to the pasta and pinto beans. Hot biscuits or dinner rolls would round out the meal nicely.

THAI-STYLE BEEF AND PEANUT SAUCE

SERVES: 4
WORKING TIME: 30 MINUTES
TOTAL TIME: 30 MINUTES

The savory peanut sauce of Thailand, commonly served with skewers of grilled meat, is a lively blend of peanut butter, chilies, coconut milk, lime juice, and a bit of fish sauce. Our version, sweetened and smoothed with honey (without the fish sauce and coconut milk), richly coats fettuccine, beef, bell pepper, and baby corn. Serve glasses of mixed tropical fruit juice as a cooling accompaniment.

10 ounces fettuccine

2 tablespoons flour

¼ teaspoon salt

½ pound well-trimmed sirloin, cut into 2 x ¼-inch strips

2 teaspoons vegetable oil

1 red bell pepper, cut into ¼-inch-wide strips

3 cloves garlic, minced

¼ cup chili sauce

2 tablespoons reduced-sodium soy sauce

2 tablespoons honey

2 tablespoons creamy peanut butter

3 tablespoons fresh lime juice

1 cup canned baby corn, rinsed, drained, and cut into 1-inch lengths

¼ cup chopped fresh basil

1. In a large pot of boiling water, cook the pasta until just tender. Drain well.

2. Meanwhile, on a sheet of waxed paper, combine the flour and salt. Dredge the beef in the flour mixture, shaking off the excess. In a large nonstick skillet, heat the oil until hot but not smoking over medium heat. Add the beef and cook, stirring, until lightly browned, about 2 minutes. Add the bell pepper and garlic and cook, stirring frequently, until the pepper is crisp-tender, about 3 minutes.

3. In a small bowl, stir together the chili sauce, soy sauce, ⅓ cup of water, the honey, peanut butter, and lime juice. Add the mixture to the skillet along with the corn and basil and bring to a simmer. Toss the sauce with the hot pasta and serve.

Helpful hint: You'll need 2 medium limes to yield 3 tablespoons of juice.

FAT: 13G/23%
CALORIES: 515
SATURATED FAT: 2.5G
CARBOHYDRATE: 75G
PROTEIN: 27G
CHOLESTEROL: 102MG
SODIUM: 764MG

CHEESY BEEF, CORN, AND TOMATO SAUCE

SERVES: 4
WORKING TIME: 30 MINUTES
TOTAL TIME: 30 MINUTES

There's a Tex-Mex twang to this family-pleasing main dish. A toss of beef, corn, and penne, united by a chunky tomato sauce, is topped with chili-flecked jack cheese. The sauce owes much of its flavor to the lacy-leaved herb, cilantro. The seeds of the plant, also known as coriander, have a peppery, citrusy taste quite different from that of the leaves. Both go into the sauce.

10 ounces medium tube pasta, such as penne rigate, penne, or ziti

3 tablespoons flour

¾ teaspoon salt

10 ounces well-trimmed top round of beef, cut into ½-inch cubes

1 tablespoon olive oil

6 scallions, thinly sliced

¾ cup reduced-sodium chicken broth, defatted

1½ cups canned no-salt-added tomatoes, chopped with their juices

¾ teaspoon ground coriander

1 cup frozen corn kernels

½ cup chopped fresh cilantro or basil

¾ cup shredded jalapeño jack cheese (3 ounces)

1. In a large pot of boiling water, cook the pasta until just tender. Drain well.

2. Meanwhile, on a sheet of waxed paper, combine the flour and salt. Dredge the beef in the flour mixture, shaking off and reserving the excess. In a large nonstick skillet, heat the oil until hot but not smoking over medium heat. Add the beef and cook, stirring frequently, until lightly browned, about 4 minutes. Add the scallions and cook, stirring frequently, until the scallions are tender, about 2 minutes. Sprinkle the reserved flour mixture over the scallions, stirring to coat.

3. Add the broth to the pan and bring to a boil. Stir in the tomatoes, coriander, corn, and cilantro and cook until the sauce is slightly thickened and the meat is cooked through, about 4 minutes. Toss the sauce with the hot pasta. Divide among 4 plates, sprinkle the cheese over, and serve.

Helpful hint: If you like your sauce spicy, a few pinches of chili powder or a few drops of hot pepper sauce would add a nice kick.

FAT: 14G/23%
CALORIES: 551
SATURATED FAT: 5.2G
CARBOHYDRATE: 72G
PROTEIN: 34G
CHOLESTEROL: 63MG
SODIUM: 719MG

SWEDISH PASTA SAUCE

SERVES: 4
WORKING TIME: 30 MINUTES
TOTAL TIME: 30 MINUTES

Cubed beets are the basis of a classic Swedish salad; the dilled sour cream sauce is also a Scandinavian inspiration.

10 ounces fettuccine

3 tablespoons flour

½ teaspoon salt

¼ teaspoon freshly ground black pepper

½ pound well-trimmed sirloin, cut into 2 x ¼-inch strips

1 tablespoon olive oil

6 scallions, thinly sliced

1½ cups cubed canned beets (½-inch cubes)

1 cup reduced-sodium beef broth

1 tablespoon Dijon mustard

2 tablespoons reduced-fat sour cream

⅓ cup snipped fresh dill

1. In a large pot of boiling water, cook the pasta until just tender. Drain well.

2. Meanwhile, on a sheet of waxed paper, combine the flour, salt, and pepper. Dredge the beef in the flour mixture, shaking off and reserving the excess. In a large nonstick skillet, heat the oil until hot but not smoking over medium heat. Add the beef and cook, stirring frequently, until lightly browned, about 2 minutes. Add the scallions and cook, stirring frequently, until the scallions are softened, about 2 minutes.

3. Add the beets to the pan, stirring to combine. In a small bowl, combine the broth and the reserved flour mixture. Stir into the skillet along with the mustard and bring to a boil. Reduce to a simmer and cook, stirring, just until the sauce is slightly thickened and no floury taste remains, about 2 minutes. Remove from the heat, stir in the sour cream and dill, and toss with the hot pasta. Divide among 4 plates and serve.

Helpful hint: Place a sheet of foil or plastic wrap over the cutting board when cubing the beets; their juice can leave indelible stains.

FAT: 10G/20%
CALORIES: 445
SATURATED FAT: 2.5G
CARBOHYDRATE: 63G
PROTEIN: 25G
CHOLESTEROL: 104MG
SODIUM: 729MG

Smothered Beef and Onion Sauce

Serves: 4
Working time: 35 minutes
Total time: 35 minutes

½ pound all-purpose potatoes, peeled and cut into ½-inch cubes

10 ounces shaped pasta, such as small shells, ruote (wagon wheels), or radiatore

1 tablespoon olive oil

2 onions, finely chopped

3 cloves garlic, minced

1 green bell pepper, cut into ½-inch squares

10 ounces well-trimmed sirloin, cut into ½-inch cubes

¾ cup reduced-sodium beef broth, defatted

¾ teaspoon salt

¾ teaspoon dried oregano

3 tablespoons grated Parmesan cheese

1. In a large pot of boiling water, cook the potatoes until firm-tender, about 4 minutes. With a slotted spoon or sieve, transfer the potatoes to a bowl; set aside. In the same pot, cook the pasta until just tender. Drain well.

2. Meanwhile, in a large nonstick skillet, heat the oil until hot but not smoking over medium heat. Add the onions and garlic and cook, stirring frequently, until the onions are soft and lightly golden, about 10 minutes. Add the bell pepper and potatoes and cook, stirring frequently, until the pepper is crisp-tender, about 4 minutes.

3. Add the beef to the pan, stirring to combine. Add the broth, salt, and oregano and cook until the meat and potatoes are cooked through, about 4 minutes. Remove ½ cup of the vegetables, transfer to a food processor, and process to a smooth purée. Return to the skillet and heat gently until the sauce is slightly thickened, about 1 minute. Toss the sauce with the Parmesan and the hot pasta, divide among 4 plates, and serve.

Helpful hint: Instead of transferring the vegetables to a food processor, you can use a hand blender right in the pot. Run the blender in 1 or 2 on/off pulses to purée about ½ cup of the vegetables, while leaving the sauce chunky.

Fat: 9g/17%
Calories: 480
Saturated Fat: 2.4g
Carbohydrate: 70g
Protein: 28g
Cholesterol: 46mg
Sodium: 651mg

This sauce is cleverly thickened by puréeing some of the vegetables rather than by adding butter or cream.

75

HAM AND RICOTTA CHEESE SAUCE

SERVES: 4
WORKING TIME: 25 MINUTES
TOTAL TIME: 30 MINUTES

We've combined green and plain fettuccine for a dish reminiscent of the classic "paglia e fieno" (straw and hay). Of course, you could use regular fettuccine alone, or spinach pasta alone, or even add rosy tomato fettuccine to echo the colors of the ham and tomatoes. Don't be deceived by the super-creamy richness of the sauce: It's made from reduced-fat cheeses.

10 ounces fettuccine, mixed colors if desired

2 teaspoons olive oil

5 ounces smoked ham, such as Black Forest or Virginia, finely slivered

⅔ cup reduced-sodium chicken broth, defatted

10-ounce package frozen chopped broccoli, thawed and drained

⅓ cup chopped fresh basil

½ teaspoon freshly ground black pepper

¾ cup low-fat (1%) cottage cheese

½ cup part-skim ricotta cheese

2 tablespoons reduced-fat cream cheese (Neufchâtel)

1 tablespoon flour

1 cup cherry tomatoes, quartered

1. In a large pot of boiling water, cook the pasta until just tender. Drain well.

2. In a large nonstick skillet, heat the oil until hot but not smoking over medium heat. Add the ham and cook, stirring occasionally, until lightly crisped, about 2 minutes. Add the broth, broccoli, basil, and pepper and bring to a boil. Reduce to a simmer and cook until the broccoli is tender, about 4 minutes.

3. In a food processor, combine the cottage cheese, ricotta, cream cheese, and flour and process to a smooth purée, about 1 minute. Add the cheese mixture to the skillet, stirring, until well combined. Add the tomatoes and cook until the sauce is thickened and the tomatoes are heated through, about 3 minutes. Toss the sauce with the hot pasta, divide among 4 plates, and serve.

Helpful hint: Black Forest ham is cured and smoked; it has an intense flavor and a dense texture. This ham is sold at most deli counters.

FAT: 11G/21%
CALORIES: 464
SATURATED FAT: 4.2G
CARBOHYDRATE: 61G
PROTEIN: 29G
CHOLESTEROL: 99MG
SODIUM: 883MG

BEEF AND MUSHROOM RAGÙ

SERVES: 4
WORKING TIME: 25 MINUTES
TOTAL TIME: 40 MINUTES

The Italian word ragù simply means a stew (think of ragoût). In culinary parlance, however, it denotes a rich, slow-cooked meat sauce. The ragùs of Bologna and Naples are quite famous: The Bolognese version is rich with butter and cream, while the Neapolitan sauce is made with red wine. Ours is an adaptation of the latter, with the addition of mushrooms.

1 tablespoon olive oil
1 onion, finely chopped
1 rib celery, finely chopped
1 carrot, finely chopped
¼ pound fresh shiitake or button mushrooms, trimmed and coarsely chopped
2 cloves garlic, minced
10 ounces medium tube pasta, such as ziti or penne
10 ounces well-trimmed top round of beef, cut into chunks
⅓ cup Marsala or dry red wine
1 cup reduced-sodium beef broth, defatted
2 cups no-salt-added canned tomatoes, chopped with their juices
¼ teaspoon salt
⅛ teaspoon red pepper flakes

1. In a large nonstick skillet, heat the oil until hot but not smoking over medium heat. Add the onion, celery, carrot, mushrooms, and garlic and cook, stirring frequently, until the vegetables are softened, about 9 minutes.

2. In a large pot of boiling water, cook the pasta until just tender. Drain well.

3. Meanwhile, in a food processor, process the meat until finely ground, about 1 minute. Add the meat to the skillet and cook until no longer pink, about 3 minutes. Add the Marsala, increase the heat to high, and cook until almost evaporated, about 2 minutes. Add the broth, tomatoes, salt, and red pepper flakes and bring to a boil. Reduce to a simmer, cover, and cook until the sauce is rich and flavorful, about 15 minutes. Divide the pasta among 4 bowls, spoon the sauce over, and serve.

Helpful hint: This sauce will freeze well. You can even package it in 4 individual portions and thaw it in the microwave as needed.

FAT: 7G/14%
CALORIES: 456
SATURATED FAT: 1.5G
CARBOHYDRATE: 68G
PROTEIN: 29G
CHOLESTEROL: 40MG
SODIUM: 369MG

Yes,
minestrone is a soup;
but it's also the ideal
inspiration for this
pasta sauce. What the
two have in common is
a bounty of vegetables
and a finishing
flourish of Parmesan.
If you have a rotary
cheese grater, bring
it—along with a
pepper mill—to the
table for customized
seasoning. Or, place
the grated cheese in a
bowl and pass it
around with the pasta.

MINESTRONE SAUCE WITH BACON

SERVES: 4
WORKING TIME: 35 MINUTES
TOTAL TIME: 35 MINUTES

10 ounces shaped pasta, such as medium shells, ruote (wagon wheels), or radiatore

2 teaspoons olive oil

¾ cup diced Canadian bacon (¼ pound)

2 ribs celery, halved lengthwise and thinly sliced

2 carrots, halved lengthwise and thinly sliced

3 cloves garlic, minced

6 ounces cabbage, cut into ½-inch chunks (see tip)

10-ounce package frozen chopped spinach, thawed and squeezed dry

2 cups no-salt-added canned tomatoes, coarsely chopped

⅔ cup reduced-sodium chicken broth, defatted

½ teaspoon dried marjoram or oregano

1½ teaspoons cornstarch mixed with 1 tablespoon water

½ cup grated Parmesan cheese

1. In a large pot of boiling water, cook the pasta until just tender. Drain well.

2. Meanwhile, in a large nonstick skillet, heat the oil until hot but not smoking over medium heat. Add the Canadian bacon and cook, stirring, until lightly crisped, about 2 minutes. Add the celery, carrots, and garlic and cook, stirring frequently, until the celery and carrots are crisp-tender, about 5 minutes.

3. Add the cabbage and spinach and cook, stirring frequently, until the cabbage is wilted, about 5 minutes. Add the tomatoes, broth, and marjoram and cook, stirring frequently, until the flavors are blended, about 5 minutes. Bring to a boil, stir in the cornstarch mixture, and cook, stirring constantly, until the sauce is slightly thickened, about 1 minute. Toss the sauce with the hot pasta, divide among 4 bowls, sprinkle the Parmesan over, and serve.

Helpful hint: You can cut up the celery, carrots, and cabbage up to 12 hours ahead of time; bag the celery and carrots together and the cabbage separately, and refrigerate until needed.

FAT: 9G/18%
CALORIES: 453
SATURATED FAT: 3.1G
CARBOHYDRATE: 70G
PROTEIN: 24G
CHOLESTEROL: 22MG
SODIUM: 791MG

TIP

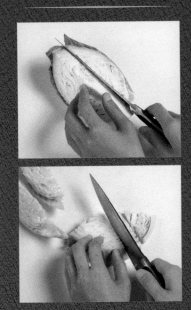

To cut a head of cabbage into chunks, first quarter the head lengthwise. Cut each quarter into 1-inch-wide wedges, then cut the wedges crosswise into ½-inch chunks.

VEGETABLE-BEEF SAUCE WITH PARMESAN

SERVES: 4
WORKING TIME: 40 MINUTES
TOTAL TIME: 40 MINUTES

Italian pastas have wonderfully literal names. Ditalini, Italian for "little thimbles," are short, straight tubes that may be either smooth or ridged. The broth-based sherry sauce used here doesn't overpower the small pasta, and the other ingredients in the dish—green peas, cubes of beef, carrot, and onion—are suitably sized to match the ditalini.

2 tablespoons flour
½ teaspoon salt
¼ teaspoon freshly ground black pepper
½ pound well-trimmed top round of beef, cut into ½-inch cubes
4 teaspoons olive oil
10 ounces small tube pasta, such as ditalini or elbow macaroni
1 onion, cut into ½-inch cubes
1 carrot, quartered lengthwise and thinly sliced
¼ cup dry sherry or white wine
1 cup reduced-sodium chicken broth, defatted
¾ teaspoon dried oregano
1 cup frozen peas
¼ cup grated Parmesan cheese

1. On a sheet of waxed paper, combine the flour, ¼ teaspoon of the salt, and the pepper. Add the beef and toss to coat, shaking off the excess. In a large nonstick skillet, heat 1 tablespoon of the oil until hot but not smoking over medium heat. Add the beef and cook until lightly browned, about 4 minutes. With a slotted spoon, transfer the beef to a plate.

2. In a large pot of boiling water, cook the pasta until just tender. Drain well.

3. Meanwhile, add the remaining 1 teaspoon oil and the onion to the skillet and cook, stirring frequently, until the onion is softened, about 7 minutes. Add the carrot and cook, stirring frequently, until the carrot is tender, about 5 minutes. Add the sherry, bring to a boil, and cook until almost evaporated, about 1 minute. Add the broth, oregano, and the remaining ¼ teaspoon salt. Bring to a boil and cook until the sauce is reduced by one-fourth, about 5 minutes. Reduce to a simmer, add the peas, and cook until the peas are heated through, about 3 minutes.

4. Transfer ½ cup of the vegetables to a food processor and process to a smooth purée. Stir the purée back into the sauce, return the beef to the pan, and cook until heated through, about 2 minutes. Toss the sauce with the hot pasta, sprinkle the Parmesan over, and serve.

FAT: 9G/17%
CALORIES: 471
SATURATED FAT: 2.4G
CARBOHYDRATE: 67G
PROTEIN: 28G
CHOLESTEROL: 36MG
SODIUM: 591MG

PORK AND PEPPER SAUCE

SERVES: 4
WORKING TIME: 35 MINUTES
TOTAL TIME: 35 MINUTES

Bright bell pepper strips, sautéed with onion and garlic, are the highlight of this easy dinner dish. Pork tenderloin gives the sauce substance; balsamic vinegar provides a gentle tang. Accompany the pasta with a tossed salad of mixed greens. Serve the salad before, with, or—Italian style—after the main course.

10 ounces shaped pasta, such as rotini, radiatore, or cavatappi

3 tablespoons flour

½ teaspoon salt

¼ teaspoon freshly ground black pepper

10 ounces well-trimmed pork tenderloin, cut into ½-inch cubes

1 tablespoon olive oil

1 onion, quartered and thinly sliced

4 cloves garlic, slivered

1 green bell pepper, cut into 1 x ¼-inch strips

1 red bell pepper, cut into 1 x ¼-inch strips

1⅓ cups reduced-sodium chicken broth, defatted

1 tablespoon no-salt-added tomato paste

2 tablespoons balsamic vinegar

1. In a large pot of boiling water, cook the pasta until just tender. Drain well.

2. Meanwhile, on a sheet of waxed paper, combine 2 tablespoons of the flour, the salt, and black pepper. Dredge the pork in the flour mixture, shaking off and reserving the excess. In a large nonstick skillet, heat the oil until hot but not smoking over medium heat. Add the pork and cook, stirring, until golden brown all over, about 4 minutes. With a slotted spoon, transfer the pork to a plate.

3. Add the onion and garlic to the pan and cook until the onion is softened, about 7 minutes. Add the bell peppers and cook, stirring, until the bell peppers are crisp-tender, about 5 minutes.

4. Sprinkle the remaining 1 tablespoon flour and the reserved dredging mixture over the vegetables, stirring to coat. Gradually add the broth, stirring until smooth and slightly thickened, about 2 minutes. Return the pork to the pan. Add the tomato paste and vinegar and cook, stirring frequently, until the sauce is thickened, and the pork is cooked through, about 1 minute. Toss the sauce with the hot pasta, divide among 4 plates, and serve.

Helpful hint: Pork should be thoroughly cooked, but overcooking will toughen it. These small cubes of meat will cook through in 4 minutes.

FAT: 7G/14%
CALORIES: 439
SATURATED FAT: 1.5G
CARBOHYDRATE: 66G
PROTEIN: 27G
CHOLESTEROL: 46MG
SODIUM: 506MG

CHUNKY TOMATO AND MEATBALL SAUCE

SERVES: 4
WORKING TIME: 30 MINUTES
TOTAL TIME: 30 MINUTES

These juicy meatballs are made with a blend of beef and pork, but for a change, you can use one or the other instead of both.

10 ounces medium strand pasta, such as spaghetti or linguine

5 ounces well-trimmed pork tenderloin, cut into chunks

5 ounces well-trimmed top round of beef, cut into chunks

¼ cup evaporated low-fat or skimmed milk

1 slice (1 ounce) firm-textured white sandwich bread, torn into small pieces

6 tablespoons grated Parmesan cheese

3 tablespoons raisins

1 egg white

½ teaspoon dried marjoram or oregano

¼ teaspoon hot pepper sauce

1 tablespoon olive oil

¼ cup flour

2 cups no-salt-added canned tomatoes, chopped with their juices

1. In a large pot of boiling water, cook the pasta until just tender. Drain well.

2. In a food processor, combine the pork and beef and process until coarsely chopped and well combined, about 30 seconds. Transfer to a medium bowl and add the evaporated milk, bread, 3 tablespoons of the Parmesan, the raisins, egg white, marjoram, and hot pepper sauce, mixing to combine well. Shape the mixture into 24 small meatballs.

3. In a large nonstick skillet, heat the oil until hot but not smoking over medium heat. Dredge the meatballs in the flour, shaking off the excess. Add the meatballs to the pan and cook, turning them as they color, until golden brown, about 3 minutes.

4. Add the tomatoes and bring to a boil. Reduce to a simmer, cover, and cook until the meatballs are cooked through, about 5 minutes. Toss the sauce with the hot pasta. Divide among 4 plates, sprinkle the remaining 3 tablespoons Parmesan over, and serve.

Helpful hint: Whenever you're making meatballs or ground-beef patties, handle the mixture lightly so the finished product will be juicy and tender. It's a good idea to mix the ingredients with two forks, tossing them gently to combine.

FAT: 10G/17%
CALORIES: 524
SATURATED FAT: 3G
CARBOHYDRATE: 75G
PROTEIN: 32G
CHOLESTEROL: 52MG
SODIUM: 274MG

SEAFOOD SAUCES

3

ajun cooks know how to show off the superb texture and flavor of just-caught seafood. Frequently the most effective treatment for fresh fish and shellfish is the simplest. Here, a light, slightly peppery, lemon sauce coats the pasta, snapper, shrimp, and bell pepper. Serve the dish with crusty garlic bread dusted with chopped parsley.

CAJUN-STYLE SEAFOOD SAUCE

SERVES: 4
WORKING TIME: 30 MINUTES
TOTAL TIME: 30 MINUTES

10 ounces shaped pasta, such as medium shells or ruote (wagon wheels)

1 tablespoon olive oil

6 scallions, thinly sliced

4 cloves garlic, minced

2 ribs celery, thinly sliced

1 green bell pepper, cut into ½-inch squares

2 tablespoons flour

1 teaspoon paprika

¼ teaspoon cayenne pepper

¼ teaspoon freshly ground black pepper

1 cup bottled clam juice or reduced-sodium chicken broth, defatted

¾ pound medium shrimp, shelled, deveined (see tip), and halved lengthwise

½ pound skinless red snapper fillets, any visible bones removed, cut into large chunks

2 tablespoons fresh lemon juice

1. In a large pot of boiling water, cook the pasta until just tender. Drain well.

2. Meanwhile, in a large nonstick skillet, heat the oil until hot but not smoking over medium heat. Add the scallions, garlic, and celery and cook, stirring frequently, until the celery is tender, about 3 minutes. Add the bell pepper and cook, stirring frequently, until the bell pepper is crisp-tender, about 3 minutes.

3. Stir the flour, paprika, cayenne, and black pepper into the pan and cook until the vegetables are well coated, about 3 minutes. Gradually stir in the clam juice and ¼ cup of water and cook, stirring frequently, until the sauce is slightly thickened and no floury taste remains, about 4 minutes. Add the shrimp, snapper, and lemon juice. Cover and cook until the fish is just opaque, about 4 minutes. Toss the sauce with the hot pasta, divide among 4 bowls, and serve.

Helpful hint: Possible substitutes for red snapper—which can be quite expensive—include flounder, cod, haddock, and rockfish.

FAT: 7G/14%
CALORIES: 462
SATURATED FAT: 1G
CARBOHYDRATE: 62G
PROTEIN: 36G
CHOLESTEROL: 126MG
SODIUM: 295MG

TIP

To shell fresh shrimp, pull apart the shell at the belly of the shrimp with your fingers, splitting the shell, and remove. To devein, with the point of a sharp knife, score the shrimp along the back, and remove the dark vein.

MEDITERRANEAN COD SAUCE

SERVES: 4
WORKING TIME: 30 MINUTES
TOTAL TIME: 35 MINUTES

In Italy, France, and Spain—countries that harvest abundant seafood along their Mediterranean coastlines—a favorite way to cook fish is with tomatoes, bell peppers, and herbs as we do here. Olive oil, garlic, and wine are often used as well. A basket of grissini (crisp, pencil-thin Italian bread sticks) would go well with this pasta dish.

10 ounces shaped pasta, such as rotini or radiatore

1 tablespoon olive oil

1 red bell pepper, cut into ½-inch squares

1 green bell pepper, cut into ½-inch squares

4 cloves garlic, minced

½ cup dry white wine

1 cup canned no-salt-added tomatoes, chopped with their juices

¾ cup bottled clam juice or reduced-sodium chicken broth, defatted

½ cup chopped fresh basil

⅓ cup chopped fresh parsley

½ teaspoon dried thyme

¾ teaspoon salt

¾ pound skinless cod fillets, any visible bones removed, cut into 1-inch chunks

1 teaspoon cornstarch mixed with 1 tablespoon water

1. In a large pot of boiling water, cook the pasta until just tender. Drain well.

2. Meanwhile, in a large nonstick skillet, heat the oil until hot but not smoking over medium heat. Add the bell peppers and garlic and cook, stirring frequently, until the bell peppers are tender, about 5 minutes. Add the wine, increase the heat to high, and cook until the wine is almost evaporated, about 4 minutes.

3. Add the tomatoes, clam juice, basil, parsley, thyme, and salt to the pan and bring to a boil. Reduce to a simmer and cook, stirring occasionally, until the flavors have blended, about 5 minutes. Add the cod, cover, return to a boil, and cook until the fish is almost cooked through, about 3 minutes. Stir in the cornstarch mixture and cook, stirring constantly, until the fish is opaque and the sauce is thickened, about 1 minute. Spoon the sauce over the hot pasta and serve.

Helpful hint: You can substitute 1 large fresh tomato or 3 plum tomatoes for the canned, if you like.

FAT: 5G/11%
CALORIES: 420
SATURATED FAT: 0.7G
CARBOHYDRATE: 62G
PROTEIN: 26G
CHOLESTEROL: 37MG
SODIUM: 573MG

*I*n

this Szechuan-inspired dish, capellini stand in for Chinese egg noodles. The pasta is topped with a colorful stir-fry of scallops, carrot, and snow peas. Most Chinese noodles take the form of long strands. Feel free to try the various types found in Chinese markets and specialty shops. You can use wheat noodles, as well as those made of buckwheat or rice.

SZECHUAN-STYLE SCALLOP SAUCE

SERVES: 4
WORKING TIME: 20 MINUTES
TOTAL TIME: 20 MINUTES

10 ounces fine strand pasta, such as capellini or spaghettini

4 teaspoons dark Oriental sesame oil

4 scallions, thinly sliced

3 cloves garlic, slivered

2 tablespoons slivered fresh ginger

2 tablespoons cornstarch

¾ pound bay scallops or quartered sea scallops (see tip)

¼ pound snow peas, trimmed and cut lengthwise into ¼-inch-wide strips

1 carrot, cut into 2 x ¼-inch julienne strips

1 cup reduced-sodium chicken broth, defatted

2 tablespoons chili sauce

¾ teaspoon salt

¼ teaspoon red pepper flakes

1. In a large pot of boiling water, cook the pasta until just tender. Drain well.

2. Meanwhile, in a large nonstick skillet, heat 2 teaspoons of the sesame oil until hot but not smoking over medium heat. Add the scallions, garlic, and ginger and cook, stirring frequently, until the scallions are tender, about 2 minutes.

3. Place all but 1 teaspoon of the cornstarch on a sheet of waxed paper. Dredge the scallops in the cornstarch, shaking off the excess. Add the remaining 2 teaspoons sesame oil to the skillet along with the scallops, snow peas, and carrot and cook, stirring constantly, until the scallops are just opaque and the vegetables are crisp-tender, about 2 minutes.

4. In a small bowl, combine the broth, chili sauce, salt, red pepper flakes, and the remaining 1 teaspoon cornstarch. Add the cornstarch mixture to the skillet and bring to a boil. Cook, stirring, until the sauce is slightly thickened, about 1 minute. Divide the pasta among 4 bowls, spoon the sauce over, and serve.

Helpful hint: The chili sauce used here is nothing exotic—just the familiar tomato-based sauce you'll find on the shelf near the ketchup at your supermarket.

FAT: 7G/14%
CALORIES: 436
SATURATED FAT: 0.9G
CARBOHYDRATE: 67G
PROTEIN: 26G
CHOLESTEROL: 28MG
SODIUM: 819MG

TIP

Tender, sweet bay scallops, no bigger across than a dime, may only be available seasonally. The larger sea scallops—about 1½ inches in diameter—are usually available year-round. If you can't find the smaller bay scallops, cut sea scallops into quarters to produce a reasonable facsimile.

SHRIMP AND FRESH SALSA SAUCE

SERVES: 4
WORKING TIME: 20 MINUTES
TOTAL TIME: 20 MINUTES

10 ounces shaped pasta, such as orecchiette or farfalle (bow ties)

1 tablespoon olive oil

4 scallions, thinly sliced

3 cloves garlic, minced

1 teaspoon minced pickled jalapeño

¾ pound medium shrimp, shelled, deveined, and halved lengthwise

¾ pound tomatoes, coarsely chopped

½ cup chopped fresh cilantro or basil

2 tablespoons no-salt-added tomato paste

1 tablespoon red wine vinegar

½ teaspoon salt

¾ cup frozen corn kernels

1. In a large pot of boiling water, cook the pasta until just tender. Drain well.

2. Meanwhile, in a large nonstick skillet, heat the oil until hot but not smoking over medium heat. Add the scallions, garlic, and jalapeño and cook, stirring frequently, until the scallions are softened, about 2 minutes.

3. Add the shrimp to the pan, stirring to coat. Add the tomatoes, cilantro, tomato paste, vinegar, and salt and bring to a boil. Reduce to a simmer, stir in the corn, and cook, stirring occasionally, until the sauce is thickened and the shrimp are just opaque, about 3 minutes. Spoon the sauce over the hot pasta and serve.

Helpful hint: This dish is best when made with juicy vine-ripened tomatoes, but the fact is you can't always get them. If necessary, substitute 1½ cups canned no-salt-added tomatoes.

FAT: 6G/13%
CALORIES: 427
SATURATED FAT: 0.9G
CARBOHYDRATE: 68G
PROTEIN: 26G
CHOLESTEROL: 105MG
SODIUM: 409MG

Shrimp cook in so little time that they are a perfect starting point for quick and easy meals. Here, the shrimp cook right in the sauce, a tangy mixture of tomatoes and corn that's brightened with garlic, jalapeño, and red wine vinegar. Be sure not to overcook this—that would toughen the shrimp and lessen the textural "bite" of the corn and fresh tomatoes.

Sole with Basil and Tomato Sauce

SERVES: 4
WORKING TIME: 30 MINUTES
TOTAL TIME: 35 MINUTES

Sole and flounder, along with their larger kin, halibut and turbot, enjoy widespread popularity, perhaps because of their mild, sweet, "unfishy" flavor. This quality also makes these fish a versatile ingredient. For a simple but delicious main dish, we've cut the fillets into chunks and simmered them in a tomato-vegetable sauce finished with a generous quantity of fresh basil.

1 tablespoon olive oil

1 onion, finely chopped

10 ounces medium strand pasta, such as linguine or spaghetti

2 carrots, quartered lengthwise and thinly sliced

2 ribs celery, quartered lengthwise and thinly sliced

½ cup dry white wine

2 cups canned no-salt-added tomatoes, chopped with their juices

1 cup bottled clam juice or reduced-sodium chicken broth, defatted

½ teaspoon salt

¾ pound sole or flounder fillets, any visible bones removed, cut into large chunks

½ cup chopped fresh basil

1½ teaspoons cornstarch mixed with 1 tablespoon water

1. In a large nonstick skillet, heat the oil until hot but not smoking over medium heat. Add the onion and cook, stirring frequently, until the onion is tender, about 7 minutes.

2. In a large pot of boiling water, cook the pasta until just tender. Drain well.

3. Meanwhile, add the carrots and celery to the skillet and cook, stirring frequently, until the carrots are crisp-tender, about 5 minutes. Add the wine, increase the heat to high, and cook until the wine is almost evaporated, about 4 minutes. Add the tomatoes, clam juice, and salt and cook, stirring occasionally, until the sauce is slightly reduced, about 4 minutes.

4. Add the sole and basil to the pan, cover, and cook until the fish is almost cooked through and the sauce is flavorful, about 3 minutes. Add the cornstarch mixture and cook, stirring constantly, until the sauce is thickened and the fish is opaque, about 1 minute. Divide the pasta among 4 bowls, spoon the sauce over, and serve.

Helpful hint: East Coast sole varieties you can use in this recipe include gray sole, winter flounder, and summer flounder; on the West Coast, petrale sole and so-called Dover sole are two options.

FAT: 6G/12%
CALORIES: 460
SATURATED FAT: 0.9G
CARBOHYDRATE: 69G
PROTEIN: 28G
CHOLESTEROL: 41MG
SODIUM: 526MG

GARLICKY COD SAUCE

SERVES: 4
WORKING TIME: 25 MINUTES
TOTAL TIME: 25 MINUTES

This aromatic sauce will delight garlic lovers in particular, but it's likely to be well received by everyone else, too: The garlic is sautéed, then simmered, so it lacks the cutting pungency of raw garlic. Reduced-fat mayonnaise creates a creamy texture that's a wonderful foil for the sauce's rich flavor. Serve a salad of tender greens and sweet red onions alongside the pasta.

10 ounces shaped pasta, such as farfalle (bow ties) or orecchiette

2 teaspoons olive oil

4 scallions, thinly sliced

8 cloves garlic, minced

2 red bell peppers, cut into ½-inch squares

10 ounces skinless cod fillets, any visible bones removed, cut into ½-inch chunks

1 cup bottled clam juice or reduced-sodium chicken broth, defatted

¼ teaspoon salt

1 cup frozen peas

3 tablespoons reduced-fat mayonnaise

⅓ cup chopped fresh parsley

1. In a large pot of boiling water, cook the pasta until just tender. Drain well.

2. Meanwhile, in a large nonstick skillet, heat the oil until hot but not smoking over medium heat. Add the scallions and garlic and cook, stirring frequently, until the scallions are tender, about 2 minutes. Add the bell peppers and cook, stirring frequently, until the bell peppers are crisp-tender, about 4 minutes. Add the cod and cook, stirring occasionally, until well coated, about 2 minutes.

3. Add the clam juice and salt to the pan and bring to a boil. Reduce to a simmer and stir in the peas, mayonnaise, and parsley. Cook, stirring occasionally, until the sauce is thickened and the fish is just opaque, about 5 minutes. Divide the pasta among 4 bowls, spoon the sauce over, and serve.

Helpful hint: For a head start, cut up the scallions, garlic, and bell peppers ahead of time and refrigerate until needed. Be sure to seal the scallions and garlic well before storing them.

FAT: 6G/13%
CALORIES: 425
SATURATED FAT: 0.9G
CARBOHYDRATE: 66G
PROTEIN: 25G
CHOLESTEROL: 31MG
SODIUM: 444MG

PROVENÇAL SHRIMP SAUCE

SERVES: 4
WORKING TIME: 35 MINUTES
TOTAL TIME: 35 MINUTES

You may recognize the ingredients for ratatouille, the Provençal vegetable dish, in this recipe. But we've expanded the scenario by adding shrimp (and pasta) to the eggplant, peppers, zucchini, and tomatoes that make a basic ratatouille. Radiatore make an especially appropriate pasta choice for this dish, since their shape slightly resembles shrimp.

10 ounces shaped pasta, such as radiatore, ruote (wagon wheels), or small shells
1 tablespoon olive oil
1 onion, finely chopped
4 cloves garlic, minced
1 small eggplant (about 8 ounces), cut into ¼-inch dice
1 red or yellow bell pepper, cut into ¼-inch squares
1 zucchini, cut into ¼-inch dice
14½-ounce can no-salt-added stewed tomatoes, chopped with their juices
2 tablespoons no-salt-added tomato paste
¾ teaspoon dried tarragon
1 teaspoon salt
¾ pound medium shrimp, shelled, deveined, and halved crosswise

1. In a large pot of boiling water, cook the pasta until just tender. Drain well.

2. Meanwhile, in a large nonstick skillet, heat the oil until hot but not smoking over medium heat. Add the onion and garlic and cook, stirring occasionally, until the onion is softened, about 7 minutes. Add the eggplant, stirring to combine. Add ½ cup of water and cook, stirring frequently, until the eggplant is tender, about 7 minutes.

3. Add the bell pepper and zucchini to the pan and cook, stirring frequently, until the bell pepper is crisp-tender, about 4 minutes. Add the tomatoes, tomato paste, tarragon, and salt and bring to a boil. Add the shrimp, reduce to a simmer, and cook until the shrimp are just opaque, about 2 minutes. Spoon the sauce over the hot pasta and serve.

Helpful hint: An eggplant might look as sturdy as a winter squash, but it's actually thin skinned and quite perishable. If you won't be using the eggplant for a day or two after buying it, store it in a plastic bag in the refrigerator.

FAT: 6G/12%
CALORIES: 447
SATURATED FAT: 0.9G
CARBOHYDRATE: 73G
PROTEIN: 26G
CHOLESTEROL: 105MG
SODIUM: 687MG

TUNA AND CREAMY MUSHROOM SAUCE

SERVES: 4
WORKING TIME: 30 MINUTES
TOTAL TIME: 35 MINUTES

*T*his lively stovetop version of the old tuna-noodle casserole, packed with flavorful fresh ingredients, is sure to please.

10 ounces shaped pasta, such as small shells, ruote (wagon wheels), or radiatore

2 teaspoons olive oil

3 tablespoons coarsely chopped Canadian bacon (1 ounce)

3 cloves garlic, minced

6 ounces mushrooms, halved and thinly sliced

2 tablespoons flour

1 cup reduced-sodium chicken broth, defatted

½ cup evaporated skimmed milk

½ teaspoon salt

½ teaspoon freshly ground black pepper

Two 6-ounce cans water-packed tuna, drained and flaked

⅓ cup grated Parmesan cheese

¼ cup chopped fresh parsley

1. In a large pot of boiling water, cook the pasta until just tender. Drain well.

2. Meanwhile, in a large nonstick skillet, heat the oil until hot but not smoking over medium heat. Add the Canadian bacon and cook until lightly crisped, about 2 minutes. Add the garlic and cook, stirring occasionally, until the garlic is softened, about 2 minutes.

3. Add the mushrooms to the pan and cook, stirring frequently, until the mushrooms are tender, about 5 minutes. Sprinkle the flour over the vegetables and cook, stirring to coat, for 1 minute. Gradually stir in the broth, evaporated milk, salt, and pepper. Bring to a boil, reduce to a simmer, and cook until the sauce is slightly thickened and no floury taste remains, about 3 minutes. Add the tuna and cook until heated through, about 3 minutes. Stir in the Parmesan and parsley.

4. Divide the pasta among 4 bowls, spoon the sauce over, and serve.

Helpful hint: Read labels carefully when buying canned tuna. Some national brands of water-packed solid white tuna have as much as 5 grams of fat in 2 ounces. Look for a brand with no more than 1 gram of fat in 2 ounces.

FAT: 7G/13%
CALORIES: 482
SATURATED FAT: 2G
CARBOHYDRATE: 63G
PROTEIN: 40G
CHOLESTEROL: 42MG
SODIUM: 951MG

SNAPPER, ASPARAGUS, AND ALMOND SAUCE

SERVES: 4
WORKING TIME: 25 MINUTES
TOTAL TIME: 25 MINUTES

10 ounces fettuccine

1 tablespoon olive oil

4 scallions, thinly sliced

1 pound asparagus, tough ends trimmed, cut on the diagonal into 1-inch lengths

¾ pound skinless red snapper fillets, any visible bones removed, cut into 1-inch chunks

¾ cup reduced-sodium chicken broth, defatted

2 teaspoons Dijon mustard

½ teaspoon salt

¼ teaspoon freshly ground black pepper

2 tablespoons reduced-fat cream cheese (Neufchâtel)

1 tablespoon fresh lemon juice

2 tablespoons slivered almonds, toasted

1. In a large pot of boiling water, cook the pasta until just tender. Drain well.

2. Meanwhile, in a large nonstick skillet, heat the oil until hot but not smoking over medium heat. Add the scallions and cook, stirring frequently, until tender, about 2 minutes. Add the asparagus, stirring to coat. Add the snapper, broth, mustard, salt, and pepper and bring to a boil. Reduce to a simmer and cook, stirring occasionally, until the fish is almost cooked through, about 4 minutes.

3. Add the cream cheese and lemon juice to the pan and cook, stirring, until the sauce is thickened and the fish is opaque, about 2 minutes. Stir in the almonds. Divide the pasta among 4 bowls, spoon the sauce over, and serve.

Helpful hint: To toast the almonds, place them in a small, ungreased skillet and cook over medium-high heat for 3 to 4 minutes, shaking the pan occasionally, until golden. Immediately tip them out of the pan onto a plate so they do not burn or scorch.

FAT: 11G/22%
CALORIES: 459
SATURATED FAT: 2.4G
CARBOHYDRATE: 57G
PROTEIN: 33G
CHOLESTEROL: 103MG
SODIUM: 550MG

For dinner-party fare in under 30 minutes, try this sophisticated sauce. Serve a raspberry sorbet for dessert.

CHILI SHRIMP SAUCE

SERVES: 4
WORKING TIME: 15 MINUTES
TOTAL TIME: 20 MINUTES

Chili is a longtime favorite for casual buffets and parties. This chili-inspired sauce, ready in a fraction of the time, is just the ticket for hungry groups. You can double the recipe as long as you possess a pot big enough to cook pasta for eight at one time. All you need to complete the meal is a great big salad and some warm rolls or bread sticks.

10 ounces small tube pasta, such as elbow macaroni or ditalini

1 tablespoon olive oil

4 scallions, thinly sliced

5 cloves garlic, minced

2 cups no-salt-added canned tomatoes, chopped with their juices

¼ cup chili sauce

½ teaspoon salt

½ teaspoon dried oregano

¾ pound medium shrimp, shelled, deveined, and cut into thirds

1. In a large pot of boiling water, cook the pasta until just tender. Drain well.

2. Meanwhile, in a large nonstick skillet, heat the oil until hot but not smoking over medium heat. Add the scallions and garlic and cook, stirring frequently, until the scallions are softened, about 2 minutes.

3. Add the tomatoes, chili sauce, and salt to the pan and bring to a boil. Stir in the oregano and shrimp, reduce to a simmer, cover, and cook until the shrimp are just opaque, about 3 minutes. Spoon the sauce over the hot pasta and serve.

Helpful hint: A sprinkling of a chopped fresh herb, such as parsley, basil, or oregano, would add extra visual appeal (and bright flavor) to the pasta.

FAT: 6G/13%
CALORIES: 419
SATURATED FAT: 0.9G
CARBOHYDRATE: 65G
PROTEIN: 25G
CHOLESTEROL: 105MG
SODIUM: 628MG

SALMON AND LEMON-DILL SAUCE

SERVES: 4
WORKING TIME: 25 MINUTES
TOTAL TIME: 30 MINUTES

10 ounces medium strand pasta, such as long fusilli, linguine, or spaghetti

2 teaspoons olive oil

2 scallions, thinly sliced

1 yellow summer squash, quartered lengthwise and thinly sliced

¼ pound smoked salmon, coarsely chopped

6 ounces skinless salmon fillet, any visible bones removed, cut into ½-inch chunks

1 cup reduced-sodium chicken broth, defatted

½ cup snipped fresh dill

1 teaspoon grated lemon zest

1 tablespoon fresh lemon juice

½ teaspoon salt

¼ cup plain nonfat yogurt

2 tablespoons reduced-fat sour cream

2 tablespoons flour

1. In a large pot of boiling water, cook the pasta until just tender. Drain well.

2. Meanwhile, in a large nonstick skillet, heat the oil until hot but not smoking over medium heat. Add the scallions and squash and cook, stirring frequently, until the squash is crisp-tender, about 4 minutes.

3. Add the smoked salmon and fresh salmon to the pan, stirring to coat. Add the broth, dill, lemon zest, lemon juice, and salt and bring to a boil. Reduce to a simmer and cook until the fresh salmon is just opaque, about 3 minutes. In a small bowl, combine the yogurt, sour cream, and flour. Add the yogurt mixture to the skillet and cook, stirring constantly, until the sauce is thickened, about 2 minutes. Divide the pasta among 4 bowls, spoon the sauce over, and serve.

Helpful hint: There are many types of smoked salmon to choose from and quite a range of prices, too. Cold-smoked Nova Scotia salmon (called "Nova") is a reasonably priced option; imported Scottish smoked salmon is considerably more expensive.

FAT: 9G/19%
CALORIES: 431
SATURATED FAT: 1.7G
CARBOHYDRATE: 61G
PROTEIN: 26G
CHOLESTEROL: 33MG
SODIUM: 680MG

This is really a double-salmon sauce, blessed with the dual richness of smoked and fresh salmon. The smoked variety—chopped to serve as a seasoning—brings intense smoky flavor to the dish; the fresh—cut into bite-size chunks—makes the pasta a satisfying meal. The creamy yogurt sauce, made with fresh lemon and dill, is a classic complement to both types of salmon.

Lime
juice, soy sauce, and
the combination of
fresh mint and basil
give this distinctive
pasta sauce its true
Thai flavor. Crisp-
tender vegetables,
including snow peas
and bamboo shoots,
provide a crunchy
contrast to the delicate
crabmeat. Spaghetti
is a suitable stand-in
for traditional Thai
rice noodles.

THAI CRAB SAUCE

SERVES: 4
WORKING TIME: 30 MINUTES
TOTAL TIME: 30 MINUTES

10 ounces medium strand pasta, such as spaghetti or linguine

1 tablespoon olive oil

6 scallions, thinly sliced

4 cloves garlic, minced

1 red bell pepper, cut into ¼-inch-wide strips

¼ pound snow peas, trimmed and cut into thin slivers

8-ounce can sliced bamboo shoots, drained

½ pound lump crabmeat, picked over to remove any cartilage (see tip)

½ cup reduced-sodium chicken broth, defatted

3 tablespoons reduced-sodium soy sauce

3 tablespoons fresh lime juice

2 tablespoons firmly packed dark brown sugar

¼ teaspoon salt

1 teaspoon cornstarch

⅓ cup chopped fresh basil

⅓ cup chopped fresh mint

1. In a large pot of boiling water, cook the pasta until just tender. Drain well.

2. Meanwhile, in a large nonstick skillet, heat the oil until hot but not smoking over medium heat. Add the scallions and garlic and cook, stirring occasionally, until the scallions are tender, about 3 minutes. Add the bell pepper and cook until crisp-tender, about 2 minutes. Add the snow peas and bamboo shoots, stirring to combine. Add the crab and cook, stirring, until heated through, about 5 minutes.

3. In a small bowl, combine the broth, soy sauce, lime juice, brown sugar, and salt. Add the cornstarch and stir until well combined. Pour the mixture into the skillet along with the basil and mint and bring to a boil. Cook, stirring constantly, until the sauce is thickened, about 1 minute. Divide the pasta among 4 plates, spoon the sauce over, and serve.

Helpful hint: Frozen snow peas may be used if fresh are unavailable.

FAT: 6G/13%
CALORIES: 431
SATURATED FAT: 0.8G
CARBOHYDRATE: 71G
PROTEIN: 24G
CHOLESTEROL: 57MG
SODIUM: 830MG

TIP

Lump crabmeat consists of large chunks of meat from the body (rather than the claws) of the crab. Before using lump crabmeat, whether fresh or canned, look it over carefully and remove any bits of cartilage or shell that may have remained in the meat. Don't over-handle the crabmeat or the "lumps" will fall apart.

LEMON CREAM WITH SPINACH AND COD

SERVES: 4
WORKING TIME: 30 MINUTES
TOTAL TIME: 30 MINUTES

Creamed spinach, accented with lemon zest, turns into a substantial pasta topping here, with the addition of chunks of cod. Frozen chopped spinach eliminates the chore of washing and stemming the spinach. And instead of butter and heavy cream, we've created a sauce using evaporated skimmed milk, part-skim ricotta cheese, and reduced-fat sour cream.

10 ounces medium strand pasta, such as perciatelli, linguine, or spaghetti

½ cup evaporated skimmed milk

¼ cup part-skim ricotta cheese

3 tablespoons reduced-fat sour cream

2 tablespoons flour

½ teaspoon salt

¼ teaspoon freshly ground black pepper

1 tablespoon olive oil

1 onion, finely chopped

10-ounce package frozen chopped spinach, thawed and squeezed dry

1 cup reduced-sodium chicken broth, defatted

1 tablespoon grated lemon zest

10 ounces skinless cod fillets, any visible bones removed, cut into large chunks

1. In a large pot of boiling water, cook the pasta until just tender. Drain well. In a food processor, combine the evaporated milk, ricotta, sour cream, flour, salt, and pepper and process to a smooth purée, about 1 minute; set aside.

2. Meanwhile, in a large nonstick skillet, heat the oil until hot but not smoking over medium heat. Add the onion and cook, stirring frequently, until softened, about 7 minutes. Add the spinach, broth, and lemon zest and bring to a boil. Add the cod, stirring to coat.

3. Add the milk mixture to the skillet and cook, stirring occasionally, until the sauce is thickened and the cod is just opaque, about 4 minutes. Divide the pasta among 4 bowls, spoon the sauce over, and serve.

Helpful hint: If you like, grate a little extra lemon zest to sprinkle over each pasta portion.

FAT: 8G/15%
CALORIES: 468
SATURATED FAT: 2.3G
CARBOHYDRATE: 68G
PROTEIN: 30G
CHOLESTEROL: 40MG
SODIUM: 573MG

MINTED SALMON SAUCE

SERVES: 4
WORKING TIME: 25 MINUTES
TOTAL TIME: 25 MINUTES

With morsels of salmon bathed in a lush cream sauce and served atop broad egg noodles, this dish suggests a sort of Stroganoff. The fresh mint, oregano, and slivered black olives, however, suggest lighter fare. For a side dish, mix up a colorful slaw of cabbage and carrots, and toss it with a citrus vinaigrette rather than a heavy mayonnaise dressing.

10 ounces wide egg noodles

1¼ cups evaporated skimmed milk

1 tablespoon flour

2 tablespoons no-salt-added tomato paste

2 teaspoons olive oil

2 cloves garlic, minced

¾ pound skinless salmon fillet, any visible bones removed, cut into 1-inch chunks

1 tablespoon reduced-fat cream cheese (Neufchâtel)

⅓ cup chopped fresh mint

½ teaspoon dried oregano

¾ teaspoon salt

¼ cup oil-cured black olives or brine-cured black olives (such as Calamata), pitted and slivered

1. In a large pot of boiling water, cook the pasta until just tender. Drain well. In a small bowl, whisk the evaporated milk into the flour. Stir in the tomato paste; set aside.

2. Meanwhile, in a large nonstick skillet, heat the oil until hot but not smoking over medium heat. Add the garlic and cook until softened, about 2 minutes. Add the salmon, stirring to coat.

3. Pour the milk mixture along with ⅓ cup of water into the skillet and bring to a simmer. Add the cream cheese, mint, oregano, and salt. Cover and cook, stirring occasionally, until the salmon is just opaque, about 4 minutes. Stir in the olives. Divide the pasta among 4 bowls, spoon the sauce over, and serve.

Helpful hint: Run your hand over the surface of the salmon to detect any tiny feather bones; if you find some, remove them with your fingers, or with tweezers or needle-nose pliers.

FAT: 14G/24%
CALORIES: 525
SATURATED FAT: 2.6G
CARBOHYDRATE: 65G
PROTEIN: 34G
CHOLESTEROL: 119MG
SODIUM: 732MG

VERACRUZ SNAPPER SAUCE

SERVES: 4
WORKING TIME: 25 MINUTES
TOTAL TIME: 30 MINUTES

This vibrant pasta dinner is an adaptation of a classic Mexican recipe. The interplay of jalapeños and citrus is irresistible.

10 ounces medium strand pasta, such as spaghetti or linguine

1 tablespoon olive oil

1 red onion, halved and thinly sliced

4 cloves garlic, minced

2 pickled jalapeños, finely chopped

Two 8-ounce cans no-salt-added tomato sauce

½ teaspoon grated orange zest

½ cup orange juice

¾ teaspoon salt

½ teaspoon dried oregano

¾ pound skinless red snapper fillets, any visible bones removed, cut into 1-inch chunks

1 tablespoon fresh lime juice

⅓ cup chopped fresh cilantro (optional)

1. In a large pot of boiling water, cook the pasta until just tender. Drain well.

2. Meanwhile, in a large nonstick skillet, heat the oil until hot but not smoking over medium heat. Add the onion, garlic, and jalapeños and cook, stirring frequently, until the onion is tender, about 7 minutes.

3. Add the tomato sauce, orange zest, orange juice, salt, and oregano to the pan and bring to a boil. Reduce to a simmer and cook, stirring occasionally, until the flavors have blended, about 4 minutes. Add the snapper and simmer until the fish is just opaque, about 4 minutes. Stir in the lime juice and cilantro. Divide the pasta among 4 bowls, spoon the sauce over, and serve.

Helpful hint: Other types of fish that will work well in this sauce include flounder, cod, haddock, and rockfish.

FAT: 6G/12%
CALORIES: 457
SATURATED FAT: 0.9G
CARBOHYDRATE: 71G
PROTEIN: 29G
CHOLESTEROL: 32MG
SODIUM: 611MG

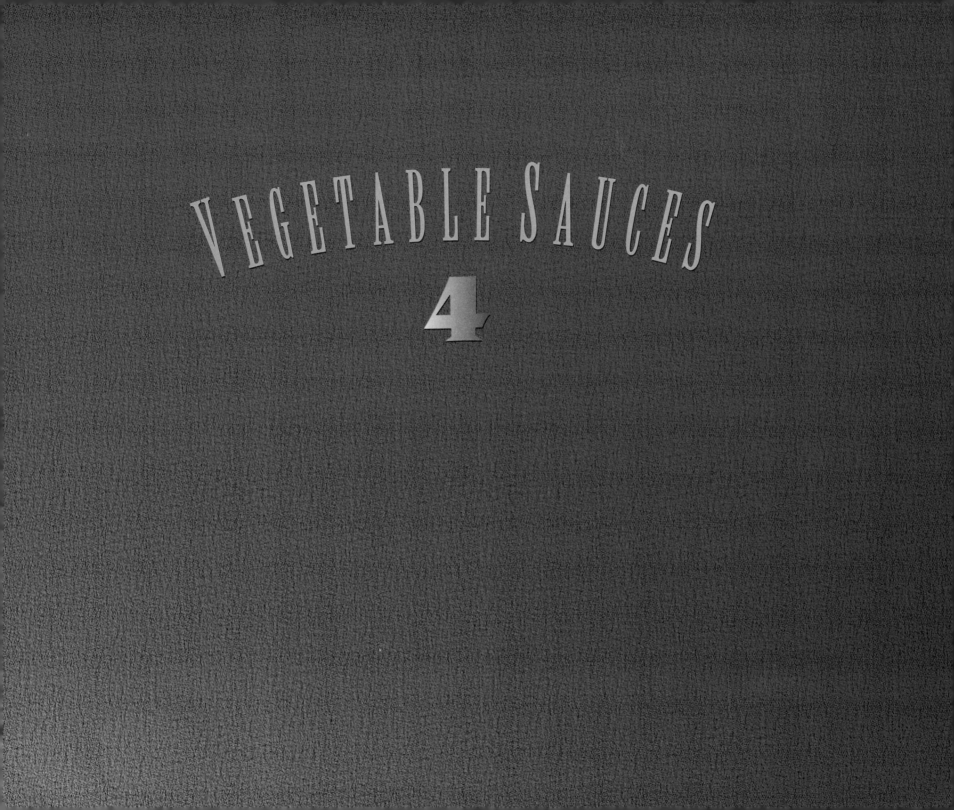

VEGETABLE SAUCES

4

MEDITERRANEAN VEGETABLE SAUCE

SERVES: 4
WORKING TIME: 20 MINUTES
TOTAL TIME: 30 MINUTES

A tomato-based topping for pasta doesn't have to be a smooth, slow-cooked sauce that takes hours to prepare. Here, for instance, fresh tomatoes are chopped and cooked for just a few minutes so they retain their shape. The tomatoes are combined with green beans, bell pepper, zucchini, and a fragrant handful of basil and tossed with a twisty-shaped pasta.

10 ounces shaped pasta, such as radiatore or rotini

4 teaspoons olive oil

1 onion, diced

2 cloves garlic, minced

¼ pound green beans, cut into 1-inch lengths

1 red bell pepper, cut into ½-inch squares

1 zucchini, quartered lengthwise and cut into ½-inch pieces

2 cups coarsely chopped fresh tomatoes, or 1½ cups canned no-salt-added tomatoes, chopped with their juices

⅓ cup chopped fresh basil

1 teaspoon salt

¼ teaspoon freshly ground black pepper

½ cup reduced-sodium chicken broth, defatted

1 tablespoon cornstarch mixed with 2 tablespoons water

1. In a large pot of boiling water, cook the pasta until just tender. Drain well.

2. Meanwhile, in a large nonstick skillet, heat 2 teaspoons of the oil until hot but not smoking over medium heat. Add the onion and garlic and cook, stirring occasionally, until the onion is softened, about 5 minutes. Add the remaining 2 teaspoons oil, the green beans, bell pepper, and zucchini. Cover and cook until the vegetables are crisp-tender, about 5 minutes.

3. Add the tomatoes, basil, salt, and black pepper to the skillet. Increase the heat to high and cook until the tomatoes are softened, about 5 minutes. Add the broth and cornstarch mixture, bring to a boil, and cook, stirring constantly, until slightly thickened, about 2 minutes. Toss the sauce with the hot pasta and serve.

Helpful hint: If the round "slicing" tomatoes in your market don't look promising, see if you can find plum tomatoes, which are meaty and, when fully ripe, deliciously sweet.

FAT: 6G/15%
CALORIES: 373
SATURATED FAT: 0.8G
CARBOHYDRATE: 69G
PROTEIN: 12G
CHOLESTEROL: 0MG
SODIUM: 639MG

SPICY TOMATO SAUCE

SERVES: 4
WORKING TIME: 25 MINUTES
TOTAL TIME: 25 MINUTES

Canned tomatoes should always be on hand in your cupboard. They're a trusty standby for sauce-making when quality fresh tomatoes aren't available. Canned tomatoes do need some dressing up, however. Here, we've added an array of highly flavorful ingredients, from Canadian bacon to capers to cayenne, for a delightfully zesty sauce.

10 ounces medium strand pasta, such as long fusilli, spaghetti, or linguine

2 teaspoons olive oil

¼ cup plus 2 tablespoons finely chopped Canadian bacon (2 ounces)

1 onion, finely chopped

4 cloves garlic, minced

1 rib celery, finely chopped

2½ cups canned no-salt-added tomatoes, chopped with their juices

¼ cup pimiento-stuffed olives, coarsely chopped

1 tablespoon capers, rinsed and drained

½ teaspoon salt

¼ teaspoon cayenne pepper

⅓ cup chopped fresh parsley

⅓ cup grated Parmesan cheese

1. In a large pot of boiling water, cook the pasta until just tender. Drain well.

2. Meanwhile, in a large nonstick skillet, heat the oil until hot but not smoking over medium heat. Add the Canadian bacon, onion, and garlic and cook, stirring frequently, until the onion is tender, about 5 minutes. Add the celery and cook, stirring frequently, until the celery is tender, about 4 minutes.

3. Add the tomatoes, olives, capers, salt, and cayenne to the pan and bring to a boil. Reduce to a simmer and cook, stirring frequently, until the sauce is richly flavored and slightly thickened, about 5 minutes. Stir in the parsley. Toss the sauce with the hot pasta and all but 2 tablespoons of the Parmesan. Divide among 4 bowls, sprinkle the remaining 2 tablespoons Parmesan over, and serve.

Helpful hint: This recipe is a good candidate to make ahead. Don't add the parsley and the remaining 2 tablespoons of Parmesan until after you've reheated the sauce for serving.

FAT: 8G/18%
CALORIES: 399
SATURATED FAT: 2.2G
CARBOHYDRATE: 65G
PROTEIN: 17G
CHOLESTEROL: 12MG
SODIUM: 892MG

One way to enhance asparagus is with its traditional partner, hollandaise sauce. But if you'd rather spare yourself the butter and egg yolks (and the tedious process of making it), try this elegant sauce, which is based on low-fat milk and reduced-fat cream cheese. It's delicately flavored with lemon, tarragon, and a touch of hot pepper sauce.

Asparagus Cream Sauce

SERVES: 4
WORKING TIME: 25 MINUTES
TOTAL TIME: 30 MINUTES

10 ounces shaped pasta, such as farfalle (bow ties) or orecchiette

2 teaspoons olive oil

1 red onion, finely chopped

¾ pound asparagus, tough ends trimmed (see tip), cut on the diagonal into 1-inch lengths

½ cup dry white wine

2 tablespoons flour

1 cup low-fat (1%) milk

1 teaspoon dried tarragon

¼ cup reduced-fat cream cheese (Neufchâtel), at room temperature

1 tablespoon fresh lemon juice

¼ teaspoon hot pepper sauce

½ teaspoon salt

3 tablespoons grated Parmesan cheese

1. In a large pot of boiling water, cook the pasta until just tender. Drain well.

2. Meanwhile, in a large nonstick skillet, heat the oil until hot but not smoking over medium heat. Add the onion and cook, stirring frequently, until softened, about 4 minutes. Add the asparagus and wine, bring to a simmer, partially cover, and cook until the asparagus is crisp-tender, about 6 minutes.

3. In a small bowl, combine the flour and milk. Add the milk mixture to the skillet along with the tarragon and cook, stirring, until thickened, about 3 minutes. Stir in the cream cheese, lemon juice, hot pepper sauce, and salt and cook, stirring, until the cream cheese is melted and the sauce is smooth, about 2 minutes. Divide the pasta among 4 bowls. Spoon the sauce over the hot pasta, sprinkle with the Parmesan, and serve.

Helpful hint: You can substitute the same amount of reduced-sodium chicken broth (defatted) for the white wine, if you like.

TIP

To prepare asparagus for cooking, hold each spear in your hands and bend it until the stem snaps off; it should break naturally where the woody base merges into the more tender part of the stalk.

FAT: 8G/17%
CALORIES: 429
SATURATED FAT: 3.4G
CARBOHYDRATE: 67G
PROTEIN: 17G
CHOLESTEROL: 13MG
SODIUM: 470MG

POTATO-SCALLION SAUCE WITH OLIVES

SERVES: 4
WORKING TIME: 25 MINUTES
TOTAL TIME: 25 MINUTES

10 ounces shaped pasta, such as rotini or radiatore

1 tablespoon olive oil

¾ pound red potatoes, cut into ½-inch cubes

4 scallions, thickly sliced

2 teaspoons dried rosemary, crumbled

4 cups coarsely diced fresh plum tomatoes, or 3½ cups canned no-salt-added tomatoes, chopped with their juices

3 tablespoons chopped green olives plus 2 teaspoons brine from the olive jar

¼ cup reduced-sodium chicken broth, defatted

½ teaspoon hot pepper sauce

¼ teaspoon salt

1. In a large pot of boiling water, cook the pasta until just tender. Drain well.

2. Meanwhile, in a large nonstick skillet, heat the oil until hot but not smoking over medium heat. Add the potatoes, cover, and cook, stirring occasionally, until they begin to brown, about 6 minutes. Add the scallions and rosemary and cook, stirring occasionally, until the potatoes are tender, about 4 minutes.

3. Stir the tomatoes into the skillet and cook until heated through, about 3 minutes. Stir in the olives, olive brine, broth, hot pepper sauce, and salt. Toss the sauce with the hot pasta and serve.

Helpful hint: The liquid (brine) from the olive jar partially salts the sauce and also intensifies the olive flavor. If you can't get 2 teaspoons of brine from the jar, use a little extra chicken broth instead.

If your "starch alarm" sounds at the thought of potatoes and pasta in a single dish, remember that carbohydrates should make up most of your daily food intake. Because the red-skinned potatoes are left unpeeled, they add an extra bit of color to the dish; for a golden touch, try Yellow Finn or Yukon Gold potatoes, which have buttery-yellow flesh.

FAT: 6G/13%
CALORIES: 415
SATURATED FAT: 0.8G
CARBOHYDRATE: 78G
PROTEIN: 13G
CHOLESTEROL: 0MG
SODIUM: 390MG

MUSHROOM-HERB SAUCE

SERVES: 4
WORKING TIME: 20 MINUTES
TOTAL TIME: 25 MINUTES

Marsala, with its richly fruity bouquet, points up the earthy flavor of the mushrooms in this delicately creamy four-vegetable sauce.

10 ounces medium strand pasta, such as spaghetti, linguine, or long fusilli

2 teaspoons olive oil

2 onions, finely chopped

2 carrots, finely chopped

2 ribs celery, finely chopped

½ pound small mushrooms, quartered

3 tablespoons Marsala or dry red wine

2 teaspoons dried basil

2 teaspoons dried rosemary, crumbled

1 cup reduced-sodium chicken broth, defatted

2 teaspoons cornstarch mixed with 1 tablespoon water

½ teaspoon salt

⅓ cup reduced-fat sour cream

3 tablespoons chopped fresh parsley

1. In a large pot of boiling water, cook the pasta until just tender. Drain well.

2. Meanwhile, in a large nonstick skillet, heat the oil until hot but not smoking over medium heat. Add the onions, carrots, and celery and cook, stirring occasionally, until the carrots are softened, about 7 minutes. Increase the heat to medium-high, add the mushrooms, Marsala, basil, and rosemary and cook until the mushroom liquid has evaporated, about 4 minutes.

3. Add the broth to the pan and return to a simmer. Stir in the cornstarch mixture and salt and cook, stirring, until slightly thickened, about 3 minutes. Remove from the heat and stir in the sour cream and parsley. Divide the pasta among 4 bowls, spoon the sauce over the hot pasta, and serve.

Helpful hint: Marsala is a fortified wine from Sicily. Use a dry Marsala for savory dishes such as this one, and save the sweeter Marsalas for desserts.

FAT: 7G/15%
CALORIES: 412
SATURATED FAT: 1.8G
CARBOHYDRATE: 72G
PROTEIN: 14G
CHOLESTEROL: 7MG
SODIUM: 467MG

PESTO WITH POTATOES

SERVES: 4
WORKING TIME: 25 MINUTES
TOTAL TIME: 35 MINUTES

2 teaspoons olive oil

½ pound red potatoes, cut into ½-inch cubes

4 cloves garlic, halved lengthwise

¾ cup reduced-sodium chicken broth, defatted

2 cups packed fresh basil leaves

¼ cup pine nuts, toasted

6 tablespoons grated Parmesan cheese

1 tablespoon fresh lemon juice

¼ teaspoon salt

¼ teaspoon freshly ground black pepper

10 ounces shaped pasta, such as orecchiette or farfalle (bow ties)

1 cup frozen peas

1. Bring a large pot of water to a boil for the pasta. In a large nonstick skillet, heat the oil until hot but not smoking over medium heat. Add the potatoes, cover, and cook, stirring occasionally, until firm-tender, about 10 minutes. Remove from the heat.

2. Meanwhile, in a small saucepan, combine the garlic and broth, bring to a simmer, and cook until the garlic is tender, about 5 minutes. Transfer to a food processor and add the basil, pine nuts, 3 tablespoons of the Parmesan, the lemon juice, salt, and pepper. Process to a smooth purée.

3. Cook the pasta in the boiling water until just tender, adding the peas during the last 1 minute of cooking. Drain well. In a large bowl, toss the pasta and peas with the pesto and potatoes. Divide among 4 plates, sprinkle the remaining 3 tablespoons Parmesan over, and serve.

Helpful hint: To toast the pine nuts, place them in a small, dry skillet and cook over medium heat, stirring and shaking the pan, for 3 minutes, or until golden. Immediately transfer the toasted pine nuts to a plate to cool.

FAT: 11G/20%
CALORIES: 491
SATURATED FAT: 2.6G
CARBOHYDRATE: 82G
PROTEIN: 21G
CHOLESTEROL: 6MG
SODIUM: 437MG

Pesto is served over a combination of pasta and potatoes here, making for an extra-hearty dish.

VEGETABLE-CHEESE SAUCE

SERVES: 4
WORKING TIME: 20 MINUTES
TOTAL TIME: 30 MINUTES

The trick to making a delicious low-fat cheese sauce is to start with a thick white sauce and then melt the cheese into it, instead of relying on the cheese itself for the desired creaminess. If the white sauce is savory and a bit spicy (ours is made with chili powder, mustard, and cayenne), you'll have a head start on flavor, and the cheese doesn't have to do all the work there, either.

10 ounces small tube pasta, such as elbow macaroni or ditalini

1½ cups evaporated skimmed milk

3 tablespoons flour

1 cup reduced-sodium chicken broth, defatted

1 teaspoon chili powder

¾ teaspoon dry mustard

⅛ teaspoon cayenne pepper

2 cups broccoli florets

1 red bell pepper, cut into ½-inch squares

2 carrots, quartered lengthwise and cut into ½-inch pieces

1 cup frozen peas

4 scallions, finely chopped

2 ounces reduced-fat cream cheese (Neufchâtel), at room temperature

1 cup shredded Swiss cheese (4 ounces)

¼ teaspoon salt

1. In a large pot of boiling water, cook the pasta until just tender. Drain well.

2. Meanwhile, in a small bowl, whisk together the evaporated milk and flour until smooth. In a large saucepan, combine the broth, chili powder, mustard, and cayenne and bring to a simmer over medium heat. Add the broccoli, bell pepper, and carrots, cover, and cook until the carrots are crisp-tender, about 5 minutes. Stir in the flour mixture and return to a simmer. Cook, stirring, until thickened and no floury taste remains, about 1 minute.

3. Stir the peas and scallions into the saucepan and cook until the scallions are softened and the peas are heated through, about 3 minutes. Remove from the heat and stir in the cream cheese, ½ cup of the Swiss cheese, and the salt until blended. Divide the pasta among 4 bowls. Spoon the sauce over the hot pasta, top with the remaining ½ cup Swiss cheese, and serve.

Helpful hint: For streamlined meal preparation, cut up the broccoli, bell pepper, and carrots up to 8 hours in advance, and refrigerate in a plastic bag until you are ready to use them.

FAT: 12G/19%
CALORIES: 577
SATURATED FAT: 6.9G
CARBOHYDRATE: 85G
PROTEIN: 32G
CHOLESTEROL: 37MG
SODIUM: 608MG

Health experts single out Fettuccine Alfredo as the most "dangerous" pasta dish of all: The sauce—simply butter, heavy cream, and Parmesan—packs an astonishing payload of fat and cholesterol. But you're perfectly safe with our pasta-and-zucchini creation. The predominant sauce ingredients are evaporated skimmed milk and part-skim ricotta cheese.

Zucchini Alfredo

SERVES: 4
WORKING TIME: 20 MINUTES
TOTAL TIME: 30 MINUTES

10 ounces medium strand pasta, such as linguine, spaghetti, or long fusilli

1 tablespoon olive oil

2 zucchini, cut into 2 x ¼-inch julienne strips (see tip)

½ cup chopped fresh basil

¾ teaspoon salt

¼ teaspoon freshly ground black pepper

¾ cup evaporated skimmed milk

½ cup part-skim ricotta cheese

¼ cup grated Parmesan cheese

1 egg

2 tablespoons flour

1. In a large pot of boiling water, cook the pasta until just tender. Drain well.

2. In a large nonstick skillet, heat the oil until hot but not smoking over medium heat. Add the zucchini, basil, salt, and pepper and cook, stirring frequently, until the zucchini is tender, about 5 minutes.

3. Meanwhile, in a blender or food processor, combine the evaporated milk, ricotta, Parmesan, egg, and flour and process until very smooth, about 1 minute. Stir the milk mixture into the skillet and cook, stirring constantly, until the sauce is piping hot and thickened, about 2 minutes. Toss the sauce with the hot pasta, divide among 4 plates, and serve.

Helpful hint: To reduce the fat even further, you can substitute low-fat (1%) cottage cheese for the ricotta,.

FAT: 10G/20%
CALORIES: 446
SATURATED FAT: 3.5G
CARBOHYDRATE: 67G
PROTEIN: 22G
CHOLESTEROL: 69MG
SODIUM: 623MG

TIP

To cut a zucchini into julienne strips, first cut the zucchini crosswise into 2-inch pieces. Then cut the pieces into ¼-inch-wide slices. Stack the slices and cut into ¼-inch-wide sticks.

Herbed Tomato Sauce

SERVES: 4
WORKING TIME: 15 MINUTES
TOTAL TIME: 20 MINUTES

The flavor of fresh herbs dissipates if they're cooked for more than a few minutes, so the tastiest sauce may well be one where they're not cooked at all. Here, basil, rosemary, and chives are stirred together with tomatoes and sautéed shallots and garlic. The herbs' flavors are released in a delicious waft of steam when you pour the sauce over the hot pasta.

2 tablespoons olive oil, preferably extra-virgin

3 shallots or 1 small onion, finely chopped

3 cloves garlic, minced

1½ pounds tomatoes, finely chopped

2 tablespoons no-salt-added tomato paste

½ cup chopped fresh basil

2 teaspoons chopped fresh rosemary, or ¾ teaspoon dried, crumbled

2 tablespoons snipped fresh chives or minced scallion greens

1¼ teaspoons salt

¼ teaspoon cayenne pepper

10 ounces medium tube pasta, such as ziti or penne

1. In a large nonstick skillet, heat 2 teaspoons of the oil until hot but not smoking over medium heat. Add the shallots and garlic and cook, stirring frequently, until the shallots are tender, about 5 minutes. Transfer to a large bowl.

2. Add the tomatoes, tomato paste, basil, rosemary, chives, salt, and cayenne to the bowl, stirring well to combine.

3. Meanwhile, in a large pot of boiling water, cook the pasta until just tender and drain well. Toss the hot pasta with the sauce and the remaining 4 teaspoons oil. Divide among 4 bowls and serve.

Helpful hint: Shallots are a member of the onion family with a mild, slightly garlicky flavor. Like garlic, shallots separate into cloves. Store shallots as you would onions, in a cool, dry place.

FAT: 9G/21%
CALORIES: 381
SATURATED FAT: 1.3G
CARBOHYDRATE: 66G
PROTEIN: 12G
CHOLESTEROL: 0MG
SODIUM: 713MG

CREAMY PRIMAVERA SAUCE

SERVES: 4
WORKING TIME: 25 MINUTES
TOTAL TIME: 30 MINUTES

Sugar snap peas are sweeter than just about any other kind of peas, but unfortunately, they have a teasingly short season. Catch them while you can and cook up a pasta dinner that celebrates the garden's bounty. Along with the peas, this dish features asparagus, carrots, and cherry tomatoes in a cream sauce light enough to let the vegetables shine through.

10 ounces shaped pasta, such as ruote (wagon wheels), medium shells, or radiatore

1 tablespoon olive oil

4 scallions, thinly sliced

3 carrots, cut into ½-inch cubes

½ pound asparagus, tough ends trimmed, cut on the diagonal into 1½-inch lengths

¼ pound sugar snap or snow peas, strings removed

1 pint cherry tomatoes, halved

½ teaspoon dried thyme

½ teaspoon salt

¼ teaspoon freshly ground black pepper

1½ cups reduced-sodium chicken broth, defatted

2 teaspoons cornstarch mixed with 1 tablespoon water

2 tablespoons reduced-fat cream cheese (Neufchâtel), at room temperature

1. In a large pot of boiling water, cook the pasta until just tender. Drain well.

2. Meanwhile, in a large nonstick skillet, heat the oil until hot but not smoking over medium heat. Add the scallions and carrots and cook, stirring occasionally, until the carrots are softened, about 5 minutes. Add the asparagus and snap peas and cook, stirring, until the asparagus is almost tender, about 5 minutes.

3. Add the tomatoes, thyme, salt, and pepper to the pan. Increase the heat to high and cook until the tomatoes are softened, about 3 minutes. Add the broth and bring to a boil. Add the cornstarch mixture and cook, stirring, until the sauce is slightly thickened, about 2 minutes. Whisk in the cream cheese until well blended. Toss the sauce with the hot pasta, divide among 4 bowls, and serve.

Helpful hint: To string sugar snap peas, pinch off the stem and pull the string from the front of the pod. If the sugar snaps are on the large side (making the strings tougher), you may want to pull the string from the back side of the pod as well.

FAT: 6G/14%
CALORIES: 386
SATURATED FAT: 1.5G
CARBOHYDRATE: 69G
PROTEIN: 15G
CHOLESTEROL: 4MG
SODIUM: 583MG

PEPPER CREAM SAUCE

SERVES: 4
WORKING TIME: 35 MINUTES
TOTAL TIME: 35 MINUTES

Sautéed bell peppers, blended into a creamy purée, make a delectable sauce for filled pasta, such as tortellini, ravioli, or agnolotti.

1¼ pounds stuffed pasta, such as (fresh or frozen) cheese tortellini or ravioli

1 teaspoon olive oil

3 red bell peppers, thinly sliced

2 yellow bell peppers, thinly sliced

1 onion, thinly sliced

1 clove garlic, sliced

½ teaspoon salt

¼ teaspoon freshly ground black pepper

½ cup reduced-sodium chicken broth, defatted

¼ cup evaporated skimmed milk

1 tablespoon no-salt-added tomato paste

1 tablespoon chopped fresh parsley (optional)

1. In a large pot of boiling water, cook the pasta until just tender. Drain well.

2. Meanwhile, in a large nonstick skillet, heat the oil until hot but not smoking over medium heat. Add the bell peppers, onion, garlic, salt, and black pepper, stirring to coat. Add the broth and cook, stirring occasionally, until the pepper mixture is very tender, about 15 minutes.

3. Transfer the pepper mixture to a food processor or blender and process to a smooth purée. Add the evaporated milk and tomato paste and process until well blended. Return the sauce to the skillet and cook over low heat until heated through, about 1 minute.

4. Toss the sauce with the hot pasta. Divide among 4 bowls, sprinkle the parsley over, and serve.

Helpful hint: Red bell peppers (especially the imported ones) can be quite expensive. If you spot some at a good price, buy a few pounds and freeze them (halved, stemmed, and cored). They'll lose their crisp texture, but they'll be fine for cooking.

FAT: 11G/20%
CALORIES: 504
SATURATED FAT: 4.4G
CARBOHYDRATE: 81G
PROTEIN: 21G
CHOLESTEROL: 59MG
SODIUM: 904MG

Artichoke-Parmesan Sauce

Serves: 4
Working time: 25 minutes
Total time: 30 minutes

10 ounces fettuccine

2 teaspoons olive oil

2 ribs celery, finely chopped

2 carrots, finely chopped

Two 9-ounce packages frozen artichoke hearts

½ cup dry white wine

½ cup reduced-sodium chicken broth, defatted

5 cups packed torn spinach leaves

4 scallions, thinly sliced

¼ teaspoon salt

⅛ teaspoon freshly ground black pepper

2 teaspoons cornstarch mixed with 1 tablespoon water

⅓ cup grated Parmesan cheese plus ½ cup shaved Parmesan

3 tablespoons reduced-fat sour cream

1 tablespoon fresh lemon juice

1. In a large pot of boiling water, cook the pasta until just tender. Drain well.

2. Meanwhile, in a large nonstick skillet, heat the oil until hot but not smoking over medium heat. Add the celery and carrots and cook, stirring frequently, until the carrots are softened, about 6 minutes.

3. Add the artichokes, wine, and broth to the pan and bring to a simmer. Cover and cook until the artichokes are tender, about 6 minutes. Stir in the spinach, scallions, salt, pepper, and corn-starch mixture. Bring to a simmer and cook, stirring, until slightly thickened, about 2 minutes.

4. Remove the pan from the heat and stir in the grated Parmesan, the sour cream, and lemon juice. Toss the sauce with the hot pasta. Divide among 4 plates, sprinkle with the ½ cup shaved Parmesan, and serve.

Helpful hints: To make Parmesan shavings, draw a vegetable peeler slowly across the side of a wedge of Parmesan. You can substitute ⅓ cup grated Parmesan for the shaved, if you like.

Fat: 12g/22%
Calories: 493
Saturated Fat: 4.4g
Carbohydrate: 73g
Protein: 24g
Cholesterol: 82mg
Sodium: 653mg

Velvety artichoke hearts jazz up this simple meal. The frozen ones are ready to use and have no added oil or salt.

PUTTANESCA SAUCE

SERVES: 4
WORKING TIME: 10 MINUTES
TOTAL TIME: 40 MINUTES

This time-honored Neapolitan sauce has many variations. Ours, which can probably be made without a trip to the grocery store, has a bold, spicy flavor—the cumulative effect of black olives, capers, anchovy paste, and red pepper flakes. Brine-cured olives make a striking difference here; if at all possible, avoid using domestic canned black olives.

1½ pounds tomatoes, coarsely chopped

⅓ cup chopped fresh parsley

¼ cup Calamata or other brine-cured black olives, pitted and finely chopped

3 tablespoons capers, rinsed and drained

2 tablespoons extra-virgin olive oil

2 tablespoons balsamic vinegar

1 tablespoon anchovy paste, or 2 tablespoons grated Parmesan cheese

1 teaspoon firmly packed light brown sugar

½ teaspoon red pepper flakes

½ teaspoon salt

10 ounces shaped pasta, such as small shells, ruote (wagon wheels), or radiatore

1. In a large bowl, combine the tomatoes, parsley, olives, capers, oil, vinegar, anchovy paste, brown sugar, red pepper flakes, and salt. Cover and let stand for 30 minutes at room temperature.

2. Meanwhile, in a large pot of boiling water, cook the pasta until just tender. Drain well.

3. Toss the sauce with the hot pasta and serve.

Helpful hints: This recipe calls for extra-virgin olive oil because the flavor of the oil is especially important in an uncooked sauce. Buy a small bottle of extra-virgin oil if you don't use it often, and store it in a cool, dark spot or in the refrigerator. You can substitute the same amount of canned no-salt-added tomatoes, with their juices, for the fresh tomatoes, if you like.

FAT: 11G/25%
CALORIES: 401
SATURATED FAT: 1.6G
CARBOHYDRATE: 64G
PROTEIN: 12G
CHOLESTEROL: 3MG
SODIUM: 778MG

Most commonly used on the Italian braised veal dish called osso buco, gremolata is a tantalizing mixture of parsley, garlic, and lemon zest: Sprinkling it over cooked food adds a burst of startlingly fresh flavor. Here, the gremolata is also used to flavor the sauce as it cooks. Follow the pasta with a bowl of fruit for a heart-healthy Italian dinner.

GREEN BEAN GREMOLATA SAUCE

SERVES: 4
WORKING TIME: 30 MINUTES
TOTAL TIME: 35 MINUTES

10 ounces medium tube pasta, such as penne rigate, penne, or ziti

1 tablespoon olive oil

¾ pound green beans, cut into 1-inch pieces

1 red onion, cut into thin slivers

½ cup chopped fresh parsley

4 cloves garlic, minced

1 tablespoon grated lemon zest (see tip)

35-ounce can no-salt-added tomatoes, chopped with their juices

¼ cup chopped fresh basil

¾ teaspoon salt

¼ teaspoon freshly ground black pepper

1 teaspoon cornstarch mixed with 1 tablespoon water

1. In a large pot of boiling water, cook the pasta until just tender. Drain well.

2. Meanwhile, in a large nonstick skillet, heat the oil until hot but not smoking over medium heat. Add the green beans and onion, cover, and cook, stirring occasionally, until the beans are crisp-tender, about 10 minutes.

3. In a small bowl, combine the parsley, garlic, and lemon zest. Add half of the parsley mixture, the tomatoes, basil, salt, and pepper to the skillet and simmer until the vegetables are tender, about 5 minutes. Add the cornstarch mixture and cook, stirring constantly, until the sauce is slightly thickened, about 1 minute. Divide the pasta among 4 plates and spoon the sauce over. Sprinkle with the remaining parsley mixture and serve.

Helpful hint: Even if you don't need it at the time, grate the zest from lemons whenever you use them. Wrap the zest and freeze it for future use.

FAT: 5G/11%
CALORIES: 400
SATURATED FAT: 0.7G
CARBOHYDRATE: 77G
PROTEIN: 14G
CHOLESTEROL: 0MG
SODIUM: 463MG

TIP

The colored outer part of citrus peel, called zest, is full of intensely flavored oils that can add a fresh zing to any dish. To remove zest, while avoiding the bitter white pith underneath, use a fine-holed grater, a citrus zester for long thin curls (pictured above, which can be chopped to approximate grating), or a vegetable peeler for wider strips that can then be thinly slivered or chopped.

ASIAN VEGETABLE-PLUM SAUCE

SERVES: 4
WORKING TIME: 25 MINUTES
TOTAL TIME: 25 MINUTES

10 ounces medium strand pasta, such as long fusilli, spaghetti, or linguine

½ cup plum jam

½ cup reduced-sodium chicken broth, defatted

2 tablespoons dry sherry

2 teaspoons dark Oriental sesame oil

1 tablespoon vegetable oil

1 clove garlic, minced

1 tablespoon minced fresh ginger

2 carrots, cut into 2 x ¼-inch julienne strips

1 red bell pepper, cut into thin strips

¼ pound snow peas, trimmed and cut into thin strips

1 cup baby corn, halved lengthwise

1 tablespoon cornstarch mixed with 2 tablespoons water

1. In a large pot of boiling water, cook the pasta until just tender. Drain well.

2. Meanwhile, in a small bowl, combine the jam, broth, ¼ cup of water, the sherry, and sesame oil.

3. In a large nonstick skillet, heat the vegetable oil until hot but not smoking over medium heat. Add the garlic and ginger and cook, stirring, until the garlic is golden, about 2 minutes. Add the carrots, bell pepper, and snow peas. Increase the heat to high and cook, stirring constantly, until the carrots are softened, about 3 minutes.

4. Add the jam mixture to the skillet along with the baby corn. Stir in the cornstarch mixture and bring to a boil. Cook, stirring, until the sauce is slightly thickened, about 2 minutes. Toss the sauce with the hot pasta, divide among 4 bowls, and serve.

Helpful hint: White wine can be substituted for the sherry, if you like.

FAT: 8G/15%
CALORIES: 484
SATURATED FAT: 0.9G
CARBOHYDRATE: 91G
PROTEIN: 12G
CHOLESTEROL: 0MG
SODIUM: 120MG

Plum sauce is a tangy Chinese condiment made from plums, chilies, vinegar, and sugar. But you don't have to go hunting for exotic ingredients, because we've created our own version of the sauce, using plum jam, broth, sherry, and sesame oil. Garlic and fresh ginger add pungency to this wonderfully unique sauce.

Neapolitan Eggplant Sauce

SERVES: 4
WORKING TIME: 35 MINUTES
TOTAL TIME: 35 MINUTES

One of the best things about eggplant is its meaty texture, which makes any dish seem more substantial. One disadvantage is its tendency to soak up every bit of oil in the pan—but that's not a problem here, since the oil in this recipe is minimal and the eggplant is simmered in broth, not fried. A touch of nutmeg and a toss of fresh mint give the vegetables a unique flavor.

10 ounces shaped pasta, such as medium shells, ruote (wagon wheels), or radiatore

2 teaspoons olive oil

1 red onion, cut into thin slivers

½ cup dry white wine

2 carrots, shredded

3 cups peeled, cubed eggplant (½-inch cubes)

½ cup reduced-sodium chicken broth, defatted

1 tablespoon no-salt-added tomato paste

4 cups coarsely diced fresh plum tomatoes, or 3½ cups canned no-salt-added tomatoes, chopped with their juices

¼ cup chopped fresh mint

¾ teaspoon salt

⅛ teaspoon nutmeg

¾ cup shredded part-skim mozzarella cheese (3 ounces)

1. In a large pot of boiling water, cook the pasta until just tender. Drain well.

2. Meanwhile, in a large nonstick skillet, heat the oil until hot but not smoking over medium heat. Add the onion and cook, stirring frequently, until softened, about 5 minutes. Add the wine and bring to a boil over medium-high heat. Add the carrots, eggplant, broth, and tomato paste and cook, stirring occasionally, until the eggplant is almost tender, about 6 minutes. Stir in the tomatoes, mint, salt, and nutmeg and cook until the tomatoes are softened, about 6 minutes.

3. Toss the sauce with the hot pasta and ½ cup of the mozzarella. Sprinkle the remaining ¼ cup mozzarella over, and serve.

Helpful hint: It's easy to peel eggplant with a swivel-bladed vegetable peeler. Cut off the stem end so that you have a cut edge of skin to start on; otherwise it can be tricky to catch the slick skin in the peeler blade.

FAT: 8G/16%
CALORIES: 450
SATURATED FAT: 2.7G
CARBOHYDRATE: 74G
PROTEIN: 18G
CHOLESTEROL: 12MG
SODIUM: 626MG

AMATRICIANA SAUCE

SERVES: 4
WORKING TIME: 30 MINUTES
TOTAL TIME: 30 MINUTES

The central-Italian valley town of Amatrice gave birth to a pasta dish now served—with variations—all over Italy. The original is a lusty dish of strand pasta sauced with a rich blend of tomatoes, bacon, and onions, liberally topped with sharp Romano cheese. Our interpretation is no less robust; brine-cured olives give it extra zip. A cool, crisp salad makes the perfect accompaniment.

10 ounces fine strand pasta, such as capellini or spaghettini

2 teaspoons olive oil

2 onions, coarsely chopped

2 cloves garlic, minced

¼ cup dry red wine

28-ounce can no-salt-added tomatoes, drained and chopped, juices reserved

¼ teaspoon red pepper flakes

¼ cup plus 2 tablespoons diced Canadian bacon (2 ounces)

2 tablespoons pitted, chopped Calamata or other brine-cured black olives

½ teaspoon salt

3 tablespoons grated Parmesan cheese

1. In a large pot of boiling water, cook the pasta until just tender. Drain well.

2. Meanwhile, in a large nonstick skillet, heat the oil until hot but not smoking over medium heat. Add the onions and cook, stirring frequently, until barely softened, about 4 minutes. Add the garlic and cook, stirring, until the garlic is softened, about 2 minutes.

3. Add the wine, the juices from the canned tomatoes, and the red pepper flakes to the skillet. Bring to a boil and cook, stirring occasionally, for 8 minutes, to thicken the sauce. Add the tomatoes, Canadian bacon, olives, and salt. Reduce to a simmer and cook until heated through, about 2 minutes. Divide the pasta among 4 plates. Spoon the sauce over the hot pasta, sprinkle with the Parmesan, and serve.

Helpful hint: If you like, you can substitute Romano for the Parmesan; it's sharper and saltier.

FAT: 7G/15%
CALORIES: 420
SATURATED FAT: 1.7G
CARBOHYDRATE: 71G
PROTEIN: 17G
CHOLESTEROL: 10MG
SODIUM: 653MG

SICILIAN CAULIFLOWER SAUCE

SERVES: 4
WORKING TIME: 20 MINUTES
TOTAL TIME: 40 MINUTES

*T*he cloud-like cauliflower florets and scalloped "gnocchi" pasta are a perfect pairing here. Tomatoes and celery add a touch of color.

⅓ cup sun-dried (not oil-packed) tomatoes

⅓ cup boiling water

10 ounces shaped pasta, such as gnocchi, radiatore, or medium shells

1 tablespoon olive oil

4 cups cauliflower florets

2 ribs celery, cut into ½-inch pieces

4 cloves garlic, coarsely chopped

¾ teaspoon fennel seeds, crushed

1 teaspoon dried basil

1 cup reduced-sodium chicken broth, defatted

⅓ cup raisins

2 teaspoons cornstarch mixed with 1 tablespoon water

⅛ teaspoon cayenne pepper

⅓ cup chopped toasted walnuts

1. In a small bowl, combine the sun-dried tomatoes and boiling water and let stand until the tomatoes are softened, about 15 minutes. Drain the tomatoes, reserving the soaking liquid. Coarsely chop the tomatoes and set aside. In a large pot of boiling water, cook the pasta until just tender. Drain well.

2. Meanwhile, in a large nonstick skillet, heat the oil until hot but not smoking over medium heat. Add the cauliflower and celery, cover, and cook, stirring occasionally, until the cauliflower is lightly browned, about 5 minutes. Stir in the garlic, fennel, and basil and cook, stirring, until the garlic is softened, about 30 seconds. Add the broth, reserved soaking liquid, sun-dried tomatoes, and raisins and simmer until the cauliflower is just tender, about 5 minutes.

3. Add ½ cup of water to the pan and bring to a boil. Stir in the cornstarch mixture and cayenne, reduce to a simmer, and cook, stirring, until the sauce is slightly thickened, about 2 minutes. Toss the sauce with the hot pasta. Divide among 4 bowls, sprinkle the walnuts over, and serve.

Helpful hint: To toast the walnuts, place them in a small, dry skillet and cook over medium heat, stirring and shaking the pan, for 3 minutes, or until golden. Immediately transfer them to a plate.

FAT: 11G/22%
CALORIES: 451
SATURATED FAT: 1.2G
CARBOHYDRATE: 76G
PROTEIN: 15G
CHOLESTEROL: 0MG
SODIUM: 187MG

Vegetable Agliata

SERVES: 4
WORKING TIME: 35 MINUTES
TOTAL TIME: 35 MINUTES

10 ounces shaped pasta, such as radiatore, farfalle (bow ties), or orecchiette

2 teaspoons olive oil

8 cloves garlic, minced

½ cup reduced-sodium chicken broth, defatted

1 cup jarred roasted red peppers, rinsed and drained

2 tablespoons no-salt-added tomato paste

1 tablespoon walnuts

1 teaspoon chili powder

⅛ teaspoon cayenne pepper

1 zucchini, quartered lengthwise and thinly sliced

1 yellow summer squash, quartered lengthwise and thinly sliced

½ cup evaporated skimmed milk

½ teaspoon salt

¼ cup chopped fresh parsley

1. In a large pot of boiling water, cook the pasta until just tender. Drain well.

2. Meanwhile, in a large nonstick skillet, heat 1 teaspoon of the oil until hot but not smoking over medium heat. Add the garlic, stirring to coat. Add the broth, cover, and cook, stirring occasionally, until the garlic is very tender, about 7 minutes. Transfer the broth mixture to a food processor along with the roasted peppers, tomato paste, walnuts, chili powder, and cayenne and process to a smooth purée.

3. In a medium skillet, heat the remaining 1 teaspoon oil until hot but not smoking over medium heat. Add the zucchini and yellow squash and cook, stirring frequently, until lightly browned and crisp-tender, about 4 minutes. Stir in the red pepper-garlic purée, the evaporated milk, and salt and bring to a boil. Reduce to a simmer and cook, stirring, until the zucchini and yellow squash are tender and the sauce is richly flavored, about 4 minutes. Toss the sauce with the hot pasta and 2 tablespoons of the parsley. Divide among 4 plates, sprinkle the remaining 2 tablespoons parsley over, and serve.

Helpful hint: You could make the roasted-pepper purée up to 8 hours in advance. Refrigerate it in a tightly closed jar so that the garlic aroma does not permeate other foods in the refrigerator.

FAT: 5G/12%
CALORIES: 367
SATURATED FAT: 0.6G
CARBOHYDRATE: 66G
PROTEIN: 14G
CHOLESTEROL: 1MG
SODIUM: 474MG

Agliata means "garlic sauce." Our interpretation is a delicious red pepper-walnut cream sauce with fresh vegetables.

BROCCOLI-TOMATO SAUCE

SERVES: 4
WORKING TIME: 35 MINUTES
TOTAL TIME: 35 MINUTES

One of the most nutritious vegetables you can eat, broccoli originated in Italy, so it's a natural for a pasta dish. Here, penne is tossed with broccoli in a hearty tomato sauce made with garlic and anchovy paste. The pasta is topped with provolone, a sweet, mellow Italian cheese that's sold sliced in most supermarkets. You could substitute smoked provolone for a change of pace.

10 ounces medium tube pasta, such as penne or ziti
2 teaspoons olive oil
2 onions, coarsely chopped
¼ cup dry sherry
1 teaspoon anchovy paste, or 1 tablespoon grated Parmesan cheese
3 cloves garlic, minced
2 teaspoons dried basil
14½-ounce can no-salt-added stewed tomatoes
8-ounce can no-salt-added tomato sauce
4 cups broccoli florets
¾ teaspoon salt
¼ teaspoon freshly ground black pepper
4 ounces thinly sliced provolone cheese, cut into 2 x ¼-inch-wide strips

1. In a large pot of boiling water, cook the pasta until just tender. Drain well.

2. Meanwhile, in a large nonstick skillet, heat the oil until hot but not smoking over medium heat. Add the onions and cook, stirring frequently, until softened, about 6 minutes. Add the sherry, anchovy paste, garlic, and basil and bring to a simmer. Cook until reduced by half, about 3 minutes.

3. Stir the tomatoes, tomato sauce, broccoli, salt, and pepper into the skillet and bring to a simmer. Cook, stirring occasionally, until the broccoli is crisp-tender, about 12 minutes. Divide the pasta among 4 plates. Spoon the sauce over the hot pasta, top with the provolone, and serve.

Helpful hint: If you like, you can top the pasta with white Cheddar, Gruyère, or Monterey jack cheese instead of provolone.

FAT: 12G/21%
CALORIES: 509
SATURATED FAT: 5.4G
CARBOHYDRATE: 77G
PROTEIN: 23G
CHOLESTEROL: 20MG
SODIUM: 774MG

Leeks, Spanish onions, and scallions are three members of the onion family that add up to a splendidly full-flavored sauce. The leek and onions are sautéed in olive oil to golden sweetness; the scallions are added toward the end of the cooking time so that they retain a touch of their fresh "green" flavor. Bread crumbs render the sauce thick and "clingy."

Three-Onion Sauce

SERVES: 4
WORKING TIME: 30 MINUTES
TOTAL TIME: 30 MINUTES

10 ounces shaped pasta, such as farfalle (bow ties) or orecchiette

1 tablespoon olive oil

1 small Spanish onion, coarsely chopped

1 leek, halved lengthwise and sliced (see tip)

½ cup reduced-sodium beef broth, defatted

4 scallions, thinly sliced

1 teaspoon dried marjoram or oregano

1½ cups coarsely chopped no-salt-added canned tomatoes

¼ teaspoon salt

¼ teaspoon freshly ground black pepper

¼ cup grated Parmesan cheese

1 slice (1 ounces) firm-textured white sandwich bread, torn into bread crumbs

1. In a large pot of boiling water, cook the pasta until just tender. Drain well.

2. Meanwhile, in a large nonstick skillet, heat the oil until hot but not smoking over medium heat. Add the onion and leek and cook, stirring occasionally, until the onion is softened and lightly golden, about 12 minutes.

3. Stir the broth, scallions, and marjoram into the skillet and bring to a boil. Reduce to a simmer and cook for 4 minutes to reduce slightly. Stir in the tomatoes, salt, and pepper and return to a simmer. Remove from the heat and stir in the Parmesan and bread crumbs. Toss the sauce with the hot pasta, divide among 4 plates, and serve.

Helpful hint: If leeks are not available, you can substitute 2 more scallions.

TIP

When a recipe calls for leeks to be sliced, first trim the root end and the dark green leaves, then cut the leeks as directed. Place the cut leeks in a bowl of tepid water, let them sit for 1 to 2 minutes, then lift the leeks out of the water, leaving any dirt and grit behind in the bowl. This is easier and faster than splitting and washing whole leeks before slicing them.

FAT: 7G/16%
CALORIES: 395
SATURATED FAT: 1.7G
CARBOHYDRATE: 70G
PROTEIN: 14G
CHOLESTEROL: 4MG
SODIUM: 374MG

SWEET PEPPER AND ONION SAUCE

SERVES: 4
WORKING TIME: 35 MINUTES
TOTAL TIME: 35 MINUTES

The warm autumn color of this hearty pasta sauce helps remind you that early fall—when red and yellow peppers are ripe for picking—is the perfect time to make this dish. The peppers are covered and cooked slowly, to concentrate their flavor. If you've made the sauce in an attractive skillet, you can use it as a serving dish: Stir the pasta into the sauce rather than vice versa.

2 tablespoons olive oil

1 onion, halved and thinly sliced

2 cloves garlic, minced

3 red bell peppers, cut into ½-inch-wide strips

2 yellow bell peppers, cut into ½-inch-wide strips

10 ounces medium strand pasta, such as long fusilli, linguine, or spaghetti

2 cups canned no-salt-added tomatoes, chopped with their juices

¾ teaspoon salt

⅓ cup chopped fresh parsley

1. In a large nonstick skillet, heat the oil until hot but not smoking over medium heat. Add the onion and garlic and cook, stirring frequently, until the onion is softened, about 7 minutes.

2. Add the bell peppers to the skillet, stir to coat, cover, and cook, stirring occasionally, until the peppers are very tender, about 15 minutes.

3. Meanwhile, in a large pot of boiling water, cook the pasta until just tender. Drain well.

4. Add the tomatoes and salt to the skillet and cook, uncovered, stirring frequently, until the sauce is richly flavored and slightly thickened, about 8 minutes. Stir in the parsley, toss the sauce with the hot pasta, and serve.

FAT: 8G/18%
CALORIES: 392
SATURATED FAT: 1.1G
CARBOHYDRATE: 69G
PROTEIN: 12G
CHOLESTEROL: 0MG
SODIUM: 438MG

GLOSSARY

Balsamic vinegar—A dark red vinegar made from the unfermented juice of pressed grapes, most commonly the white Trebbiano, and aged in wooden casks. The authentic version is produced in a small region in Northern Italy, around Modena, and tastes richly sweet with a slight sour edge. Balsamic vinegar adds a pleasant tang to pasta sauces.

Basil—A highly fragrant herb with a flavor somewhere between licorice and cloves. Like many fresh herbs, basil will retain more of its taste if added at the end of cooking; dried basil is quite flavorful and can stand up to longer cooking. Store fresh basil by placing the stems in a container of water and covering the leaves loosely with a plastic bag.

Canadian bacon—A lean smoked meat, similar to ham. This bacon is precooked, so it can be used as is. (For extra flavor, cook it in a skillet until the edges are lightly crisped.) Just a small amount adds big flavor to sauces and soups, but with much less fat than regular bacon.

Capers—The flower buds of a small bush found in Mediterranean countries. To make capers, the buds are dried and then pickled in vinegar with some salt: To reduce saltiness, rinse before using. The piquant taste of capers permeates any sauce quickly, and just a few supply a big flavor boost.

Cayenne pepper—A hot spice ground from dried red chili peppers. Add cayenne to taste when preparing Mexican, Tex-Mex, Indian, Chinese, and Caribbean dishes; start with just a small amount, as cayenne is fiery-hot.

Cilantro/Coriander—A lacy-leaved green herb (called by both names). The plant's seeds are dried and used as a spice (known as coriander). The fresh herb, much used in Mexican and Asian cooking, looks like pale flat-leaf parsley and is strongly aromatic. Store fresh cilantro by placing the stems in a container of water and covering the leaves loosely with a plastic bag. Coriander seeds are important in Mexican and Indian cuisines; sold whole or ground, they have a somewhat citrusy flavor that complements both sweet and savory dishes.

Cornstarch—A fine flour made from the germ of the corn. Cornstarch, like flour, is used as a fat-free sauce thickener; cornstarch-thickened sauces are lighter, glossier, and more translucent than those made with flour. To prevent lumps, combine cornstarch with a cold liquid before adding it to a hot sauce; bring it gently to a boil and don't stir too vigorously or the sauce may thin.

Cream cheese, reduced-fat—A light cream cheese, commonly called Neufchâtel, with about one-third less fat than regular cream cheese. It can be used as a substitute for regular cream cheese. A small amount used in sauces duplicates the richness of full-fat cheese or heavy cream.

Curry powder—Not one spice but a mix of spices, commonly used in Indian cooking to flavor a dish with sweet heat and add a characteristic yellow-orange color. While curry blends vary (consisting of as many as 20 herbs and spices), they typically include turmeric (for its vivid yellow color), fenugreek, ginger, cardamom, cloves, cumin, coriander, and cayenne pepper. Commercially available Madras curry is hotter than other store-bought types.

Dill—A name given to both the fresh herb and the small, hard seeds that are used as a spice. Add the light, lemony, fresh dill leaves (also called dillweed) toward the end of cooking. Dill seeds provide a pleasantly distinctive bitter taste and marry beautifully with sour cream- or yogurt-based sauces.

Evaporated milk, skimmed and low-fat—Canned, unsweetened, homogenized milk that has had most of its fat removed: In the skimmed version, 100 percent of the fat has been removed; the low-fat version contains 1 percent fat. Used in sauces, these products add a creamy richness with almost no fat. Store at room temperature for up to 6 months until opened, then refrigerate for up to 1 week.

Garlic—The edible bulb of a plant closely related to onions, leeks, and chives. Garlic can be pungently assertive or sweetly mild, depending on how it is prepared: Minced or crushed garlic yields a more powerful flavor than whole or halved cloves. Whereas sautéing turns garlic rich and savory, slow simmering or roasting produces a mild, mellow flavor. Select firm, plump bulbs with dry skins; avoid bulbs that have begun to sprout. Store garlic in an open or loosely covered container in a cool, dark place for up to 2 months.

Hot pepper sauce—A highly incendiary sauce made from a variety of hot peppers flavored with vinegar and salt. This sauce comes into play in Caribbean and Tex-Mex dishes as well as Creole and Cajun cuisines. Use sparingly, drop by drop, to introduce a hot edge to any dish.

Jalapeño peppers—Hot green chili peppers about two inches long and an inch in diameter, with rounded tips. Most of the heat resides in the membranes (ribs) of the pepper, so remove them for a milder effect—wear gloves to protect your hands from the volatile oils. Jalapeños are also sold whole or chopped in small cans, although the canned version is not nearly as arresting as the fresh. Toss a little jalapeño into soups, sautés, baked dishes, or anywhere you want to create some fire.

Juice, citrus—The flavorful liquid component of oranges, lemon, limes, tangerines, and the like. Freshly squeezed citrus juice has an inimitable freshness that livens up low-fat foods. Frozen juice concentrates make a tangy base for sweet or savory sauces. An inexpensive hand reamer makes quick work of juicing citrus fruits.

Marjoram—A member of the mint family that tastes like mildly sweet oregano. Fresh marjoram should be added at the end of the cooking so the flavor doesn't vanish. Dried marjoram, sold in leaf and ground form (the more intense leaf being preferable), stands up to longer cooking.

Marsala—A sweet, nutty, fortified wine made in Sicily. To make Marsala, sweet concentrated grape juice is added to strong white wine; the wine is then aged for several years and, in some cases, blended. Marsala is much used in cooking: Sweet Marsala is good for dessert-making, but a dry version should be used in savory sauces.

Milk, low-fat—Liquid whole milk that contains between .5 and 2 percent milk fat. This type of milk is great for enriching sauces—it adds just a small fraction of the fat found in cream. However, with 2 to 4 grams of fat per cup, low-fat milk is not a good choice for adults to drink (stick with skim milk).

Olive oil—A fragrant oil pressed from olives. Olive oil is one of the signature ingredients of Italian cuisine. This oil is rich in monounsaturated fats, which make it more healthful than butter and other solid shortenings. Olive oil comes in different grades, reflecting the method used to refine the oil and the resulting level of acidity. The finest, most expensive oil is cold-pressed extra-virgin, which should be reserved for flavoring uncooked or lightly cooked sauces. "Virgin" and "pure"

olive oils are slightly more acidic with less olive flavor, and are fine for most types of cooking.

Olives—Small, oval fruits native to the Mediterranean region with an intense, earthy taste. Olives are picked green (unripe) or black (ripe) and then must be cured—in oil or brine—to mellow their natural bitterness and develop their flavor; herbs and other seasonings are added to create a wide variety of olives. Spanish olives—green olives sold whole, pitted, or pimiento-stuffed—add jazzy color as well as piquant flavor. The Calamata, a purple-black, brine-cured olive, is a full-flavored Greek-style olive that works well in pasta sauces. Use all olives sparingly since they are high in fat (olive oil).

Onions, red—Medium- to large-sized spherical onions with purplish-red skins. Red onions are somewhat milder than yellow or white globe onions; they don't require long cooking to mellow their flavor, so they're perfect for briefly cooked (or uncooked) sauces. Bermuda onions or Spanish onions can be substituted for red onions.

Oregano—A member of the mint family characterized by small, green leaves. Prized for its pleasantly bitter taste, oregano is essential to many Mediterranean-style dishes and is used in Mexican cooking as well.

Parmesan cheese—An intensely flavored, hard grating cheese. Genuine Italian Parmesan, stamped "Parmigiano-Reggiano" on the rind, is produced in the Emilia-Romagna region, and tastes richly nutty with a

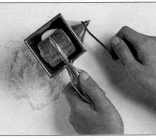

slight sweetness. Buy Parmesan in blocks and grate it as needed for best flavor and freshness. For a fine, fluffy texture that melts into hot foods, use a hand-cranked grater.

Parsley—A popular herb available in two varieties. Curly parsley, with lacy, frilly leaves, is quite mild and is preferred for garnishing, while flat-leaf Italian parsley has a stronger flavor and is better for cooking. Store parsley as you would basil. Since fresh parsley is so widely available, there is really no reason to use dried, which has very little flavor.

Peppercorns, black—The whole dried berries of a tropical vine, *piper nigrum*. A touch of this hot, pungent seasoning enlivens just about any savory dish, and the flavor of freshly ground pepper is so superior to pre-ground that no cook should be without a pepper grinder filled with peppercorns.

Peppers, bell—The large, sweet members of the Capsicum family of vegetables. Green bell peppers are most common; red peppers have ripened and are sweeter. You can also buy yellow, orange, purple and brown bell peppers in some markets. Choose well-colored, firm peppers that are heavy for their size; these will have thick, juicy flesh. Store peppers in a plastic bag in the refrigerator for up to a week. Before preparing bell peppers, remove the stem, spongy ribs, and seeds.

Red pepper flakes—A spice made from a variety of dried red chili peppers. Pepper flakes will permeate a sauce or stew with a burst of heat and flavor during the cooking and eating. Begin with a small amount—you can always add more.

Rosemary—An aromatic herb with needle-like leaves and a sharp pine-citrus flavor. Rosemary's robust flavor complements lamb particularly well, and it stands up to long cooking better than most herbs. If you can't get fresh rosemary, use whole dried leaves, which retain the flavor of the fresh herb quite well. Crush or chop rosemary leaves with a mortar and pestle or a chef's knife.

Scallions—Immature onions (also called green onions) with a mild and slightly sweet flavor. Both the white bulb and the green tops can be used in cooking; the green tops make an attractive garnish. To prepare, trim off the base of the bulb or root end and any withered ends of the green tops. Remove the outermost, thin skin from around the bulb. Cut the white portion from the green tops and use separately, or use together in the same dish.

Sour cream—A soured dairy product, resulting from treating sweet cream with a lactic acid culture. Regular sour cream contains at least 18 percent milk fat by volume; reduced-fat sour cream contains 4 percent fat; nonfat sour cream is, of course, fat-free. In cooking, the reduced-fat version can be substituted for regular sour cream; use the nonfat cautiously since it behaves differently in some types of recipes. To avoid curdling, do not subject sour cream to high heat.

Sun-dried tomatoes—Plum tomatoes that have been dried slowly to produce a chewy, intensely flavorful sauce ingredient. Although oil-packed tomatoes are widely available, the dry-packed type are preferred for their lower fat content. For many recipes, the dried tomatoes must be soaked in hot water to soften them before using.

Thyme—A lemony-tasting member of the mint family frequently paired with bay leaves in Mediterranean-style dishes and rice-based preparations. The dried herb, both ground and leaf, is an excellent substitute for the fresh.

Tomato paste—A concentrated essence of cooked tomatoes, sold in cans and tubes. Tomato paste is commonly used to thicken and accent the flavor and color of sauces; however, it is slightly bitter and should not be used alone or in large quantities. Cooking tomato paste mellows it. If you're using only part of a can of tomato paste, save the remainder by freezing it in a plastic bag.

Tomato sauce—A cooked, seasoned purée of fresh tomatoes, sold in cans or jars. Tomato sauce is usually seasoned with salt, spices, and corn syrup; some brands come in Italian- or Mexican-style versions with more assertive flavorings. The recipes in this book call for "no-salt-added" tomato sauce, because the regular sauce is quite high in sodium.

Tomatoes, canned—Fresh tomatoes processed and packed for easy use and reliable year-round quality. Canned tomatoes are definitely preferable when the only available fresh tomatoes are hard, pale, and lacking in flavor. Canned whole peeled plum tomatoes, often imported from Italy, are especially tasty; they can be packed with or without added salt and are sometimes packed with herbs. You can also buy canned crushed tomatoes, packed with no added liquid, or with tomato juice, purée, or paste. The recipes in this book call for "no-salt-added" tomatoes. Some no-salt-added brands are not labeled as such—check the ingredient list.

Tomatoes, cherry—Round tomatoes roughly the size of ping-pong balls; may be red or yellow. These bite-size tomatoes add a colorful touch to pasta dishes and are great for salads. Cherry tomatoes are usually sold in baskets. Choose well-colored specimens and store them at room temperature to preserve their flavor.

Tomatoes, plum—Smallish, egg-shaped or oblong tomatoes. Sometimes called Roma tomatoes, these are meatier (thicker fleshed, with less liquid inside) than most globe tomatoes, which makes them excellent for cooking. They are a good choice when vine-ripened local tomatoes are not available.

Tomatoes, stewed—Canned tomatoes that have been cooked with seasonings and other vegetables, such as onions, green peppers, or celery. Stewed tomatoes add an extra touch of flavor to pasta sauces, soups, and stews.

Wine, dry white—A non-sweet alcoholic beverage made from fermented grape juice. White wine may be made from white grapes, or from red grapes with their skins and seeds removed. Dry white wine lends a unique fragrance and flavor to sauces. Avoid the so-called "cooking wines" sold in supermarkets: These are of poor quality and may have added salt. Instead, buy an inexpensive but drinkable white. Once opened, recork and refrigerate the bottle.

Yogurt, nonfat and low-fat—Delicately tart cultured milk products made from low-fat or skim milk. Plain yogurt adds creamy richness (but little or no fat) to pasta sauces. Be careful when cooking with yogurt, as it will curdle if boiled or stirred too vigorously: Adding flour or cornstarch to the yogurt before adding it to a hot sauce helps stabilize it.

Zest, citrus—The thin, outermost colored part of the rind of citrus fruits that contains strongly flavored oils. Zest imparts an intense flavor that makes a refreshing contrast to the richness of meat, poultry, or fish. Remove the zest with a grater, citrus zester, or vegetable peeler; be careful to remove only the colored layer, not the bitter white pith beneath it.

INDEX

TIME LIFE BOOKS

Time-Life Books is a division of Time Life Inc.

TIME LIFE INC.

PRESIDENT and CEO: George Artandi

TIME-LIFE BOOKS

PRESIDENT: John D. Hall
PUBLISHER/MANAGING EDITOR: Neil Kagan

GREAT TASTE-LOW FAT
Pasta Sauces

DEPUTY EDITOR: Marion Ferguson Briggs
MARKETING DIRECTOR: Cheryl D. Eklind

Consulting Editor: Catherine Boland Hackett

Vice President, Director of Finance: Christopher Hearing
Vice President, Book Production: Marjann Caldwell
Director of Operations: Eileen Bradley
Director of Photography and Research: John Conrad Weiser
Director of Editorial Administration (Acting): Barbara Levitt
Production Manager: Marlene Zack
Quality Assurance Manager: James King
Library: Louise D. Forstall

Design for Great Taste-Low Fat by David Fridberg of
Miles Fridberg Molinaroli, Inc.

REBUS, INC.
PUBLISHER: Rodney M. Friedman
EDITORIAL DIRECTOR: Charles L. Mee

Editorial Staff for *Pasta Sauces*
Director, Recipe Development and Photography: Grace Young
Editorial Director: Kate Slate
Senior Recipe Developer: Sandra Rose Gluck
Recipe Developers: Helen Jones, Paul Piccuito, Marianne Zanzarella
Writer: Bonnie J. Slotnick
Managing Editor: Julee Binder Shapiro
Editorial Assistant: James W. Brown, Jr.
Nutritionists: Hill Nutrition Associates

Art Director: Timothy Jeffs
Photographer: Lisa Koenig
Photographer's Assistants: Alix Berenberg, Katie Bleacher Everard,
   Rainer Fehringer
Food Stylists: Karen Tack, Karen Pickus
Assistant Food Stylists: Charles Davis, Ellie Ritt
Prop Stylist: Debrah Donahue
Prop Coordinator: Karin Martin

Library of Congress Cataloging-in-Publication Data

Pasta sauces.
   p.   cm. -- (Great taste, low fat)
Includes index.
ISBN 0-7835-4563-0
1. Sauces. 2. Low-fat diet--Recipes. 3. Quick and easy cookery.
I. Time-Life Books. II. Series.
TX819.A1P37 1997
641.8'22--dc21   96-44017
                                                  CIP

OTHER PUBLICATIONS

COOKING
WEIGHT WATCHERS® SMART CHOICE RECIPE COLLECTION
WILLIAMS-SONOMA KITCHEN LIBRARY

DO IT YOURSELF
THE TIME-LIFE COMPLETE GARDENER
HOME REPAIR AND IMPROVEMENT
THE ART OF WOODWORKING
FIX IT YOURSELF

TIME-LIFE KIDS
FAMILY TIME BIBLE STORIES
LIBRARY OF FIRST QUESTIONS AND ANSWERS
A CHILD'S FIRST LIBRARY OF LEARNING
I LOVE MATH
NATURE COMPANY DISCOVERIES
UNDERSTANDING SCIENCE & NATURE

HISTORY
THE AMERICAN STORY
VOICES OF THE CIVIL WAR
THE AMERICAN INDIANS
LOST CIVILIZATIONS
MYSTERIES OF THE UNKNOWN
TIME FRAME
THE CIVIL WAR
CULTURAL ATLAS

SCIENCE/NATURE
VOYAGE THROUGH THE UNIVERSE

*For information on and a full description of any of the Time-Life Books series
listed above, please call 1-800-621-7026 or write:*
Reader Information
Time-Life Customer Service
P.O. Box C-32068
Richmond, Virginia 23261-2068

METRIC CONVERSION CHARTS

VOLUME EQUIVALENTS
(fluid ounces/milliliters and liters)

US	Metric
1 tsp	5 ml
1 tbsp (½ fl oz)	15 ml
¼ cup (2 fl oz)	60 ml
⅓ cup	80 ml
½ cup (4 fl oz)	120 ml
⅔ cup	160 ml
¾ cup (6 fl oz)	180 ml
1 cup (8 fl oz)	240 ml
1 qt (32 fl oz)	950 ml
1 qt + 3 tbsps	1 L
1 gal (128 fl oz)	4 L

Conversion formula
Fluid ounces X 30 = milliliters
1000 milliliters = 1 liter

WEIGHT EQUIVALENTS
(ounces and pounds/grams and kilograms)

US	Metric
¼ oz	7 g
½ oz	15 g
¾ oz	20 g
1 oz	30 g
8 oz (½ lb)	225 g
12 oz (¾ lb)	340 g
16 oz (1 lb)	455 g
35 oz (2.2 lbs)	1 kg

Conversion formula
Ounces X 28.35 = grams
1000 grams = 1 kilogram

LINEAR EQUIVALENTS
(inches and feet/centimeters and meters)

US	Metric
¼ in	.75 cm
½ in	1.5 cm
¾ in	2 cm
1 in	2.5 cm
6 in	15 cm
12 in (1 ft)	30 cm
39 in	1 m

Conversion formula
Inches X 2.54 = centimeters
100 centimeters = 1 meter

TEMPERATURE EQUIVALENTS
(Fahrenheit/Celsius)

US	Metric
0° (freezer temperature)	-18°
32° (water freezes)	0°
98.6°	37°
180° (water simmers*)	82°
212° (water boils*)	100°
250° (low oven)	120°
350° (moderate oven)	175°
425° (hot oven)	220°
500° (very hot oven)	260°

*at sea level

Conversion formula
Degrees Fahrenheit minus
32 ÷ 1.8 = degrees Celsius